Rudy's Stories

Rudy Martin Jr.

Copyright © 2024 Rudy Martin Jr.
All rights reserved
First Edition

Fulton Books
Meadville, PA

Published by Fulton Books 2024

ISBN 979-8-89221-044-7 (paperback)
ISBN 979-8-89221-045-4 (digital)

Printed in the United States of America

The 1957 Miss Arkansas Contest

By Rudy Martin Jr.

The 1957 Miss Arkansas Beauty Pageant was held in Mariana, Arkansas, starting Friday night.

At the end of the spring semester, I was dating a girl (Carolyn Sorrells) from Hughes, which is not far from Mariana.

Everybody calls her Sorrels.

She invited me to spend the weekend with her and her parents and to come Thursday night if possible.

I got a ride from Pine Bluff to Mariana on Thursday afternoon, and Sorrels was waiting on me.

A bunch of U of A students from around there planned to go "juking" Thursday night at the "Plantation Inn" nightclub in West Memphis. They have a really good rock and roll singing group, and Sorrels is an excellent dancer!

The plan was for the kids who lived around Hughes to meet at seven on Thursday night at Steve Bernard's house. I knew him from school.

Sorrel's mother fixed an excellent dinner for us.

Her father graciously offered to let us use their car so we wouldn't be dependent on someone else.

When it was time to go, Mr. Sorrels opened the door
from the kitchen to the garage, "gently" pushed us
into a pitch-black garage and shut the door.

I barely got a glimpse of their car, but I saw enough
to know it was a late-model Chevrolet!

Sorrels handed me the keys, and I got them in the ignition.

In the dark, I couldn't tell if it was a stick
shift or automatic transmission.

I didn't want to be too obvious feeling for
the clutch, so I turned the key.

I guessed wrong. The car lurched forward, and the grill banged
into all kinds of what sounded like tools and other things!

With that, Mr. Sorrels turned the light in the garage on
and opened the door to see what was going on.

All of the windows were down, and all I could think of to
say was, "Sorry, I thought it was automatic transmission!"

He said, "Okay" and closed the door.

Sorrels directed me to Steve's house, and we were the first
ones there. It was set back from the highway about a hundred
yards, and you got to the house by a built-up "road."

Soon a bunch of kids arrived and went inside.

A record player was playing rock and roll music,
but there wasn't enough room to dance.

Steve announced that it was time to leave,
so everybody got into their cars.

Of course, everybody drove to Steve's house facing it.
Now they had to back down the built-up road!

They must have been there before, because nobody
had any trouble transversing the road.

When everybody had left but me, Steve said that he had
a spotlight on his car and he would direct me with it.

I made a bad assumption!

I assumed that he would show me where to go
with his spotlight, but he shined the light where he
didn't want me to go, so I drove into a ditch!

He pulled me out of the ditch with a small tractor,
and we followed him to the Plantation Inn.

Everybody had a great time there.

When it came time to leave, Sorrels said she wanted me to
take her to Horseshoe Lake to park and "pet" there!

We were into some serious petting when we realized
we were getting eaten alive by mosquitoes!

We agreed that the petting would have to
wait, and I took us to her house.

On Friday, Sorrels showed me around Hughes, Marianna,
West Memphis, and Forrest City. There wasn't much to see.

However, we did some big-time petting on an isolated
road behind the Mississippi River levee!

The plan was for us to ride to and from
the contest with Teddy Gilbert.

We were on our way when I told a joke and banged my
hand on the window glass behind Teddy and it shattered!

I apologized profusely and said I would pay to get it
fixed, but he said for me not to worry about it.

The contest was fun for me for a while, but I got bored.

Teddy was bored too, so he took us to Sorrel's
house, and we called it a night.

The next morning, Sorrel's brother and his wife
were there, along with their son, Charles.

They called him Chogie!

Chogie was all decked out in his Western gear—ten-
gallon hat, cowboy boots, double pistols, etc.

I love kids, so I started playing cops and robbers with him.

His pistols were cap guns, so I "died" a bunch of times!

He got grouchy, so his mother put him
in her lap and he settled down.

I was sitting in a high-back chair reading the paper
when unbeknown to me or his parents, he pulled a stool
behind my chair, climbed up on it, pulled out one of
his pistols, and cracked me over the head with it!

I saw stars!

Before I knew it, I had pulled Chogie over my head and had him suspended over my lap.

Chogie screamed bloody murder as blood ran down the front of my shirt!

His mother jumped up, grabbed Chogie, and put him in her lap, where he quieted down.

Sorrels went and got me a Band-Aid, and Chogie's parents apologized over and over for what he did.

I graciously said it was okay, but it wasn't!

When I got home, my mother asked me if I had a good time. I said, "I don't want to talk about it!"

Bent Over

By Rudy Martin

I had been fishing in a pond near Gillette and was heading home.

I was pulling Dad's lightweight aluminum boat on my trailer.

I got into a tremendous storm as I reached Tucker—thunder, lightning, etc.

I was driving into the wind as I approached England, and a huge puff of wind bent the boat over backward! I heard the bow scraping the pavement!

It was getting dark, and I was standing on the shoulder of the road trying to figure out what I was going to do with the boat when a car pulled over and stopped.

Four young Black men got out and approached me.

One of them said, "Sir, it looks like you're in a heap of trouble. Can we help you?"

They took the boat off of the trailer and left it in a field.

I thanked them profusely and handed them a twenty-dollar bill. They said, "No, sir. We won't accept your money. We're just glad we could help you!"

I put the $20 bill into the hand of the man I had been talking to and said, "I saw a liquor store back towards Sherrill. Go there and get you boys some whiskey!"

The guys in the car started whooping and hollering, turned around, and headed straight for the liquor store!

Bifocals

By Rudy Martin

A man and his wife went to the eye doctor's office to pick up some bifocals he had ordered earlier.

When they called his name, he went with the nurse, and he stayed and stayed and stayed!

He finally came into the waiting room, and he had a great big wet spot on his pants!

His wife got him to sit by her, and she asked him what happened.

He said, "I put on these new bifocals, and on the way back to you, I had to pee.

And while I was admiring that great big one, the little one peed all over me!"

The people in the waiting room gave him a standing ovation!

Black Label

By Rudy Martin

I played tennis for the Razorbacks—lettered three years.

The coach was a man named Red Davis.

Bill Tedford and I were the Mark Twains of the SAE house.

I found out that Red would give us a fifth of Black Label for a dozen frog legs!

We commenced to scour the countryside for frogs and were quite successful!

Bill and I had rented a duplex near the campus, and each of us had two full fifths of Jack Daniel and a partially full fifth on our chest of drawers!

My dad came up to Fayetteville, and we proudly showed him our duplex.

Dad took one look at our chest of drawers and said, "Men, there are cheaper whiskeys than Black Jack Daniel, and you don't have to buy three fifths apiece at a time!"

We told him about the deal we had with Red, and he said, "Times a-wasting. Let's go tonight!"

Blouse

By Rudy Martin

My cousin Currin Nichol married a woman named
June Cross. She taught me English in junior high.

They lived right next to a doctor named Bob Crawford and
his wife. Dr. Bob was an eye, ear, nose, and throat doctor.

They were the best of friends, and Bob and June
often played practical jokes on each other.

June had an appointment with him, and when she finished,
he followed her into the waiting room, talking.

The waiting room was packed, and when she was leaving (Dr. Bob
was still there), June said in a loud voice, "Dr. Crawford, my ears
are a lot better, but I'm curious as to why you took my blouse off!"

Of course, everybody in the waiting room
was laughing their head off!

Dr. Bob tripped trying to get out of there, and
the people there clapped for him!

Brooks Robinson

By Rudy Martin

When I was in high school, I was dating
a cute girl named Connie Ellis.

One Sunday afternoon, I decided to drive
up there unannounced and see her.

When I got to her house, there was a two-
door black car in front of her house.

My feathers fell!

I thought that Connie and I were getting along great,
but it looked like I had been shot out of the saddle!

I rang the doorbell, and this nice-looking
young man answered the door.

It was Brooks Robinson, great basketball player and future
all-pro baseball player for the Baltimore Orioles!

I quickly got the hell out of dodge and drove home!
Three years later, I was in Fayetteville to
watch a Razorback football game.

I was walking up a ramp to get to my seat when lo and
behold, Brooks Robinson was walking down the ramp!

He instantly recognized me and said, "Rudy Martin, how are you doing?"

How in the world did he recognize me when he had met so many people?

Colonel

By Rudy Martin

I was taking basic training at Lackland Air Force Base in San Antonio, Texas.

The man who was in charge of giving calisthenics took a shine to me and asked me if I would take over that job.

I said yes, but calisthenics was right before a class I was required to attend, so I had to really hustle.

I finished my calisthenics class and only had my jockstrap on when I saw movement and an officer's cap with scrambled eggs on it!

I snapped to attention wearing only my jockstrap when I heard, "Tenhutt!"

A Colonel stepped into my room and just about died laughing!

He said, "Cadet, why did you come to attention when I entered your room?"

I said I attended Culver Summer School in Culver, Indiana, for eight weeks for three summers in a row, and they told us to snap to attention anytime an officer entered our room. "You are an officer, so I snapped to attention!"

He said, "Good job, cadet!"

Truck Driver

By Rudy Martin

A truck driver walked into a truck stop, sailed his hat across the room, looked at the waitress, and said, "I want a pot of coffee, a dozen eggs scrambled, a pound of bacon and a pot of coffee now!"

The patrons in the restaurant murmured some, then went back to their meal.

Three hippies came in just as his meal came out; and they intercepted it and put it on their table!

That made the patrons really murmur!

The truck driver didn't say a word, got up, paid his check, and left!

The hippies ate his meal and said to the cashier, "That truck driver wasn't much of man, was he?"

The cashier said, "And I guess he isn't much of a truck driver either. I saw him drive over three motorcycles as he left the parking lot!"

Turpentine

By Rudy Martin

Growing up, my grandmother Nannie would come stay with my sister and me when my folks were out of town.

When I was a teenager, I taught myself to do taxidermy. I mounted ducks, geese, squirrels, fish, and frogs.

Doing taxidermy required that I use very sharp tools like scalpels.

Nannie was with us, and I cut my hand pretty badly with a scalpel! It was bleeding a lot!

She wrapped my hand in a towel and took me to the backyard so I wouldn't bleed in the house.

Outside, she poured some Mercurochrome on it, but it didn't stop the bleeding.

So she went into Dad's barn and came out with a bottle of turpentine!

She warned me that it was going to burn, and boy, did it!

She poured a big dose of it on the gash, and I started yelling "Oh, it burns! Oh, it burns," and running around the yard.

It finally quit burning, and the bleeding stopped, so Nannie wrapped my hand with gauze.

I couldn't do any taxidermy for two weeks!

But He Did

By Rudy Martin

It was drizzling rain, and there was no
moon. It was pitch-black dark!

A man was taking a shortcut through a cemetery, when
all of a sudden, he stepped in an open grave!

The hole was about six feet deep, and the sides were muddy.

He tried to climb out for a few minutes, then realized that he would
have to wait for the backhoe people to get him out in the morning.

Pretty soon, a Black man was also taking a shortcut
when he slid into the opposite end of the grave from the
other man, and he too started trying to climb out!

After a few minutes, the original man who fell in
tapped the Black man on the shoulder and said,
"Excuse me, sir, but you can't get out of here!"

But he did!

Cadaver Dog

By Rudy Martin

My lifelong friend at one time owned a retriever kennel in Grand Junction, Tennessee. They trained dogs to win field trials.

He sold it and started training cadaver dogs.

He was very good at it and went to work for the sherriff's department.

Recently his dog had found a man's body in twelve feet of water!

When 9/11 happened, he was stationed at the pentagon and he told me that the only thing his dog found was part of a human scalp!

One night, he showed me what cadaver dogs do.

He had been to several dentist's offices to get the teeth they had pulled, and he put them in a metal ammunition box.

It was nighttime. He put a leash on his dog, handed him to me, and told me not to move.

He disappeared into the darkness for about ten minutes and came back without the can.

I don't remember the command he gave his dog, but the dog took off running into the darkness!

He said that his dog was to find the can, sit down, and bark once!

In about twenty minutes, we heard a single bark, and my friend said, "He's got it!"

Sure enough, there he was, sitting beside the open can!

What a nose!

Capers

By Rudy Martin

My wife and I were having marital problems, so we went to see a marriage counselor. We talked for about an hour, and each of us got to express our feelings.

He said, "I don't hear any real problems, but I think that part of your problems revolve around your sex life."

"I don't want you to have sex for sixty days!"

"Sixty days! We can't do that!"

"Yes, you can. Now do it!"

They met again in thirty days, and the counselor said, "How did y'all do?"

"Well, we lasted fifty-nine days!"

"We were eating dinner, and my eyes met hers, my hand touched her hand, my knee touched her knee, and *wham*, we went to the floor and did it right beside the table!"

The counselor said, "So how are y'all getting along now?"

The man said, "We're getting along great, but we can't eat at Capers Restaurant anymore!"

The Carrol Burnett Show

By Rudy Martin

The Carol Burnett Show was always super funny. Carol would try to make a cast member (Harvey Korman) laugh, and he would try not to laugh.

It was hilarious!

There was another person on the show, and his name was Tim Conway. He would also try to get Harvey to laugh when he didn't want to.

It was hilarious!

On one show, Tim played a dentist. He told Harvey he did not go to dental school. First, he had Harvey lie down in the dentist's chair and asked him to open his mouth wide.

Tim took one look and told Harvey that the tooth that was sore would have to come out!

Harvey protested loudly, but to no avail!

Tim got a "tooth puller" and pulled and twisted that sore tooth until it came out!

Harvey jumped up out of the dentist's chair and ran round and around the room yelling in pain!

Tim told Harvey that he'd forgotten to deaden it and proceeded to deaden both of his own hands!

That was enough for Harvey—he jumped up out of the dentist's chair and ran out of the room screaming in pain!

Don Lusby

By Rudy Martin

Andy Payne, Henry Trotter, and I duck hunted a lot in high school.

As my dad would say, "Henry is so tight he won't even pay attention!" or, "Henry is so tight he won't even spend the day!"

We would eat breakfast there before the hunt. Henry never had any money in his wallet, and he always wrote a check for the exact amount of his breakfast!

Another quirk he had was that he always wrote another check for the exact amount of a box of shotgun shells! And he never had any left over from the previous hunt!

Donald Budge

By Rudy Martin

Henry Trotter and his wife Sue went on
a cruise on their honeymoon.

Henry has a very good ping-pong player, and on the
second day, he found a table on the second level.

The custom for ping-pong is that the winner
keeps playing until he loses.

He told me that he had beaten a number of players when
an elderly gentleman asked him if he could play.

Of course, Henry said "yes," and the elderly
gentleman proceeded to beat him "21–0."

They talked afterward, and the elderly gentleman said his name
was Donald Budge, arguably the best tennis player ever!

Going Up

By Rudy Martin

I was going through basic training at Lackland Air Force Base in San Antonio, Texas.

We were housed in barracks, and the base often had fire drills.

That meant that no matter what, everybody had to get out of the barracks.

A crusty first sergeant named Charlie Tedford was in charge of our barracks.

Late one night, the alarm sounded, and everybody made a mad dash for the door.

The sergeant was calling the roll, and when he got to "Livingston," there was dead silence!

He wasn't there!

So the sergeant had to look in every room to see where he was hiding.

He searched every room and decided that Livingston must be hiding in the closet we used to hang up our uniforms.

He was searching the end room on the second floor, and when he opened the closet, there was airman Livingston!

Airman Livingston sheepishly said, "Going up?" and Sergeant Tedford almost died laughing and said, "Good job, Airman!"

King Sparrow

By Rudy Martin

When I was in grade school, I had a Benjamin pump BB gun. It could be pumped up, and the more you pumped it, the harder it shot.

When I shot a regular Red Ryder BB gun, it only bounced off a Coke can, but when I shot it with my Benjamin pump pumped only three times, the BB went through both sides of the can!

Dad wouldn't let me pump it but three times, but that was plenty for even a pigeon!

Each afternoon when I got home from school, I changed into my hunting clothes and shell vest and toured the alleys behind the houses in my neighborhood.

Dad had warned me that he would take my Benjamin away from me if he found out that I was also shooting songbirds (mockingbirds, robins, cardinals, brown thrashers, etc.).

One day, I had particularly good luck, and my mother yelled for me to come in—supper was ready.

I hurried in, washed my hands and face, and enjoyed a delicious meal.

My bedroom was the last one, and I could get to the screened-in-porch and out that door into the backyard.

Dad and I shared a bathroom, and I had a closet back there.

One day, my mother took Dad back to my room, and it was obvious that something was dead (and ripe) back there.

Dad searched the closet and came up with my shell vest, which had five dead sparrows in it!

He was not a happy camper and made me carry them in my hands to the garbage cans!

No Brakes

By Rudy Martin

Four of us got in my car at the SAE house to go somewhere. There was a pretty steep hill where the road crossed Arkansas Avenue.

When I pushed the brake pedal to slow down, it went all the way to the floor. I panicked!

Everybody in the car was yelling, "Stop! Stop! Stop!"

As we crossed Arkansas Avenue, I spied a tennis court with a metal net.

Meanwhile, everybody in the car was yelling for me to stop!

I aimed my car for the middle of the net, and it came to an abrupt stop!

I never did understand why those four men would never ride with me again.

No Groceries

By Rudy Martin

Until they moved out onto Olive Street, the Ford Dealership was at Fifth and State Street, just behind Simmons Bank at Fifth and State.

For some reason, Henry Trotter Jr. took a shine to my father, Rufus Martin, who worked at Simmons Bank. Henry called him "Brother Martin."

Henry would come into the bank about nine each morning, and he and my dad would drink coffee and visit.

One morning Henry told Dad that a senior vice president of Ford Motor Company wanted to come to Arkansas to go duck hunting for a weekend. And he would like to bring another senior officer.

We had a nice clubhouse on little Lennox Lake near Dumas, Arkansas, and there was plenty of room to house everyone.

Their arrival date was two weeks away, and Henry spent every morning with Dad making lists of the groceries they would be needing—eggs, bacon, sausage, biscuits, steaks, etc.

The Executives arrived on a Friday morning, and we all headed for the clubhouse. Dad looked in Henry's station wagon and couldn't find any groceries!

Henry looked sheepish and said he forgot to buy them.

So Dad and Henry headed for a grocery store in Dumas. When it came time to pay, Henry didn't have any money!

Cheapskate!

No Poncho

By Rudy Martin

When the Razorbacks played TCU in Fayetteville in 1960, it was raining cats and dogs.

Before we went downstairs for the spaghetti lunch at the SAE House, I put three ponchos on my bed.

When I came up to get them, there were only two there, with a note from Tommy Stobaugh saying, "Rudy, I saw that you had three ponchos out and didn't think you would need one of them for the game, so I took one!"

I was not a happy camper, but my dad and uncle had come up for the game, so I got soaking wet and Tommy stayed dry for the game, which we won three to nothing when Freddy Akers kicked a field goal as time expired.

I don't remember exactly what I said to Tommy, but some canines were mentioned!

No Trucks

By Rudy Martin

A Texas Aggie was finishing up his boot camp training by parachuting out of an airplane.

The rough, tough sergeant was briefing the men on what to expect.

The door was open, and the sergeant said, "Men, this will be easy for you.

I'll push you out the door, you count to ten and pull your rip cord.

If the main chute doesn't open, count to ten again and pull your auxiliary rip cord.

The trucks will be at the landing area to take you to your barracks."

The sergeant pushed the Aggie out of the plane. The Aggie counted to ten, and the main chute didn't open.

He counted to ten again, and the auxiliary chute didn't open either!

Of course, the Aggie was hurtling toward the ground!

He looked down and said, "I guess the trucks won't be there either."

Not Even Pregnant

By Rudy Martin

A woman was walking around the Pentagon with a baby in her arms and a toddler holding her hand.

A security guard came up to her and said, "Lady, there are signs all over the Pentagon saying, 'No children allowed!'"

She narrowed her eyes at him and said, "Let me tell you one thing. When I first got lost in this place, I wasn't even pregnant!"

Not Vacant

By Rudy Martin

I went to work for IBM after I graduated from college.

Computers were just coming on the scene, so my branch manager sent me to St. Louis for six weeks to learn how to write programs.

I was assigned the third shift supervisor in the data center.

Customers were coming from all over the country to learn how to program, and my job was to show them how.

I did a good job!

When I got back to Memphis, they had a 1401 computer installed on the second floor.

It was only going to be there for three weeks, so another IBMer and I were burning the midnight oil teaching customers with 1401's on how to program them.

I had no sleep for two days, so the branch manager rented a room in the Holiday Inn next door for us.

But when I unlocked the door, it flew open, and this giant of a man said, "Who in the hell are you? This is our room!"

I saw his wife scoot by in her slip!

I apologized and got the hell out of Dodge!

I decided to play a practical joke on the
other IBMer that was helping me.

He showed up a little while later, and I told him how
much better I felt after a nap and a shower.

He hadn't been gone ten minutes when he
appeared and started cussing me out!

Evidently, the man in the room threatened the man
in the room and threatened my friend with bodily
harm! He didn't speak to me for a week!

Oak Hall

By Rudy Martin

I went to work for IBM in Memphis when I graduated from college.

I had heard that IBM had a very serious dress code, and right before I started, I got a letter from the Branch Manager there that told me what clothes I need to be wearing when I met him.

The letter read:

Buy the following things at Oak Hall downtown men's store:

Three-piece suit complete with a vest

Black Florsheim wing tip shoes

Modest tie

Briefcase

Business hat

I went there. They were friendly, and I got everything I needed.

A friend back home said I looked like an FBI agent.

On the Creek Bank

By Rudy Martin

One year a genius graduated from Harvard Law School.

IBM has a think tank at their corporate office in Endicott, New York, and they were eager to get the genius in it.

They took him into a big room that had a very large computer in it.

They told him that this was the most powerful computer in the world.

They said that you can ask it any question, and you do that by writing your question on a 3 × 5 index card and feeding it into the slot.

They said that the computer would spit out the answer on a 3 × 5 index card.

The young man wrote, "Where is my father?" on the card and put it in the slot.

The computer blinked its lights just a few seconds and spit out a card that said, "Your father is on the creek bank fishing."

The young man said, "That's not the correct answer—my father died three years ago!"

The think tank men huddled for about thirty minutes and asked the young man if he could rephrase the question.

So the young man wrote, "Where is the man my mother married?"

The computer blinked its lights just a few seconds and spit out a card that said, "The man your mother married died three years ago, but your father is on the creek bank fishing!"

One Last Shot

By Rudy Martin

Dad died when he was eighty-two, after an extended battle with prostate cancer.

Predictably, he fought the good fight.

His last duck hunt was about eighteen months before his death.

It was a Saturday in January of 1985. By then, Dad's cancer had spread into his bones, and according to him, it was very painful most of the time.

I brought my fourteen-year-old son Al, and we met Dad at the lake.

It was a clear, cool day, and we hunted the west blind, one that wasn't hunted very often.

Things were pretty slow, but we managed to kill four ducks by eight o'clock.

Around nine, he told me that his arms were really hurting, and he needed me to take him to his car.

Al and I decided that we would stay for a while.

I unloaded my gun and got into the boat, which was under the boat hide behind the blind.

As Dad was unloading his gun, I heard the unmistakable quacks of a hen mallard.

I eased back into the blind, and sure enough, we
spotted her circling our decoys with locked wings.

As I "talked" to her with my call, she made a couple
of high passes, then committed to our spread.

As she came into range, Dad rose and made a picture-perfect shot
with his weathered Winchester Model 50 semiautomatic 12 gauge.

We all exchanged high-fives as my lab, Suzie, made the retrieve.

Of course, none of us knew at the time that that
was the last shot he would ever fire.

He lasted through another duck season,
but his hunting days were over.

Even today, that final scene is still vivid in
my mind. I will cherish it always.

Just in the last few weeks, I have realized an all-too-obvious
fact: my biological clock is ticking, and my time left on
this earth is far less than the time that's already expired.

If I live to be as old as he was, I've got nineteen years left.

I've been blessed with extraordinary health, but one never knows.

Wouldn't it be déjà vu if somewhere down the road, my
son and his son watch me kill the last duck I shoot at?

Dad, I love you and miss you!

I can't wait to join you in heaven!

Ouch!

By Rudy Martin

A redneck country man had a sore tooth and went to the dentist.

The dentist looked at it and said he would have to pull it, and the country man said okay.

But when the dentist held the syringe up, the country man jumped out of the chair and started yelling, "Whoa, you're not sticking me with that needle!"

The dentist said, "You can't take it without deadening it!"

The country man said, "I'm not going to let you stick me with that needle!"

The dentist argued with the country man for a while and said, "Okay, but it's really going to hurt!"

The dentist pulled the tooth, and the country man jumped out of the chair and started yelling, "That hurts, that really, really hurts!"

The country man said, "But I can think of two things that hurt me worse than that!

I was bird hunting and I had to take a crap.

I tied my dog up, pulled my pants down, and squatted over a bear trap, and it snapped right on my balls!"

The dentist said, "You said that there were two things that hurt you worse than that. What was the other one?"

The country man said, "That's when I hit the end of the chain!"

Out

By Rudy Martin

A Texas Aggie was deer hunting and got lost. He sat down, leaned against a tree, and smoked a cigarette.

He waited about thirty minutes and said to himself, "I went to a one-week class on what to do if you're lost, and they said that the international distress signal is to fire three shots into the air and wait for somebody to come."

So he stood up and fired three shots into the air and sat back down.

No response.

He waited another thirty minutes, stood up, fired three more shots into the air, and sat back down.

No response.

He waited another thirty minutes, stood up, fired three more shots into the air, and sat back down.

Still no response.

He waited another thirty minutes, stood up, fired three more shots into the air, and sat back down.

Still no response

He said, "If this keeps up, I'll be running out of arrows!"

Pakistan

By Rudy Martin

A friend of mine was going through underwater demolition training in Rhode Island when he met and became friends with a man from Pakistan.

He taught this man the hog call—"Whooooo pig soooooie, whooooo pig soooooie, whooooo pig soooooie, razorbacks!"

The man finished the class and went back to Pakistan, and my friend was stationed on a destroyer.

Two years later, my friend's destroyer docked in Pakistan for a week.

As he was walking down the gang plank, he heard, "Whooooo pig soooooie, whooooo pig soooooie, whooooo pig soooooie, Razorbacks!"

It was his friend!

Pawpaw Jelly

By Rudy Martin

My grandmother (Ms. Suzie Martin) was born in
Magnolia, Arkansas. It's a quaint little town.

Her maiden name was Keith, and there were lots of Keiths there.

She told me that when she was growing up, her dad
would take her to Bodcau Bayou to gather pawpaw berries
so her mother could fix them some pawpaw jelly.

Pawpaw bushes grow along the bank of Bodcau Bayou.

The berries were red, and they floated, so she used
a dip net with fine mesh to scoop them up.

Her mother taught her how to make it, and
she sold it to neighbors and friends.

My parents loved it (and so did all of the members
of the Martin clan), so she brought a lot of bottles
of it when she came to visit. It was delicious!

I haven't seen a jar of it in years, but I'd give a
pretty penny just to taste it one more time!

Peach Days

By Rudy Martin

My wife was born in a small town in Oklahoma, then her family moved to Brigham City, Utah, when she was in the sixth grade. She graduated from high school there.

Every year, Brigham has Peach Days. It lasts a week.

It's "a happening!"

On the last day, they have a parade, complete with a marching band, floats, cheerleaders, old cars, etc.

We were there three years in a row.

Unfortunately, the first year Mary broke her ankle when we were touring the state capitol in Salt Lake.

Mary was a "Trooper," and I wheeled her all-over Utah and Wyoming in a wheelchair!

Although there are lots of mountains around, there are many peach orchards around, and they produce the best-tasting peaches in the world.

That's what we go out there for!

We had them for every meal, and Mary, her friend Saundy, and I ate a whole peach cobbler for a snack!

We always stayed at the Sheraton Hotel, which was downtown. They had a very good free buffet breakfast every morning, and that's how we started our day!

One morning, I decided I wanted a waffle.

I wasn't sure how to do it, but I found a waffle maker, poured waffle batter in it, turned it on, and got some scrambled eggs with sausage while my waffle was cooking.

I checked it a couple of times and was putting it on my plate when a woman who was behind me said, "Sir, that's my waffle!"

I didn't notice that there were two waffle makers when I got over there.

I had put the batter in one of them and was taking the one that was done out of the other one, and that one belonged to the woman who said, "Sir, that's my waffle!"

Mary kidded me about that for years!

Mary and I:

Visited Yellowstone for a week.

Saw Old Faithful.

Saw the hot bubbling pools.

Drove through a snowstorm in July.

Saw the Grand Tetons and Jackson Hole, Wyoming.

Rode the ski lift at Robert Redford's ranch.

Saw Salt Lake.

Sat in the Mormon tabernacle in Salt Lake
and marveled at the acoustics.

Visited where the railroad from the east met the
one from the west and rode the train there.

Toured the Utah State campus and toured a wildlife sanctuary.

She showed me the drugstore she worked
in when she was in high school.

Mary, thank you for giving us seven fabulous years together!

I will always love you.

We will always have Kate's Love, "The Couch," "The Couch," "The Couch," Brigham City and Yellowstone.

I will always love you.

Give me a call sometime if it feels right.

Rudy
(501) 747-0824

Pecker

By Rudy Martin

My wife was a first grade school teacher for
many years. She absolutely loved it!

She told me that one day, she was at the chalkboard
when she saw the teacher next door frantically
waving for her to come out in the hall.

She did, and the teacher was doubled over in laughter. She
said her kids' assignment was to use crayons to color various
creatures—lions, tigers, elephants, birds, fish, etc.

The teacher said that little Johnny came up to her
and showed her the toucan he was coloring.

He said, "Ms. Jones, I've colored everything but his pecker.

What color should I use for that?"

Pigeons

By Rudy Martin

Henry Trotter and I grew up together, and we were always up to something. He lived in a four-story house.

I was spending the night with him, and we decided to try to catch a pigeon that roosted right by his second story bedroom with a Dip Net.

We got out on the tile roof, and the pigeons panicked!

One brushed Henry's shoulder. He lost his balance and almost fell off the roof!

We decided that discretion was the better part of valor and retreated to his bedroom!

Possible

By Rudy Martin

When I was in high school, my dad had hernia
and hemorrhoid surgeries at the same time. He
was in the old Davis Hospital in Pine Bluff.

I visited him every day, and he said he was really sore!

One day when I came in, he was really laughing!

He said that his nurse was an overweight, grumpy
nurse, and she came in this morning and said
that she was going to give him a bath.

He said she washed him to below his navel and up to
his crotch and said, "I've washed down as far as possible
and as far up as possible. Now you wash possible!"

Quiet Flakes

By Rudy Martin

Some of the best duck-hunting trips I've had
were when it was sleeting and snowing.

The weatherman was forecasting both sleet and snow
in the afternoon, so I was itching to get out there.

I called several friends, but they were tied
up, so I set out on my own.

When I reached Pipkin Lake the wind was howling
from the north and making whitecaps!

I was considering heading for the house when I saw several
hundred ducks working the west end of the lake.

That convinced me to go!

I bailed out the boat, pushed off from the bank, and
the 5hp outboard started on the third pull.

Waves were splashing over the bow of the boat. When I saw that it
was relatively calm right up against the bank, I idled to the blind.

I secured the boat in the boat hide and stepped into
the blind with my shotgun and shell box.

Hundreds of ducks were milling around the
blind and landing in my decoys.

I loaded my gun and quickly killed two mallard drakes.

Then a mallard hen showed up right over the decoys, an easy shot.

Unfortunately I crippled her. She sailed about
thirty yards past the decoys and went down.

She was out of range, so I jumped in the boat,
started the motor, and took off after her.

When there's only one person in a johnboat and he's sitting
on the back seat, all the water in the boat rushes to the back
of the boat, especially when you're running a motor!

I knew I was in a dangerous situation—waves were washing over the
stern and quickly filled the boat with water almost to the gunwales!

I shut the motor off, grabbed my shotgun, crawled on my
knees to the middle seat, and sat on it facing forward.

The boat was so full of water that the slightest
move made it almost roll over!

I figured out that I needed to be absolutely still and
let the wind take me where it wanted to.

The snow was really coming down, and I
realized that it was eerily quiet.

The wind blew me into a line of willow
trees on the south side of the lake.

I could see some stalks of milo about fifteen yards
from where I was, so I knew it was shallow there.

I slowly pivoted the front of the boat ninety degrees and used the
willow trees to pull the boat through them, and when the bow
touched the bottom of the lake, I let out a yell—I was saved!

I stepped out of the boat and turned it on its side to pour the water out of it, slid it back into the water, put my gear in it, started the motor, and headed across the lake to my car.

Then I thanked the man upstairs for saving my life!

Rabbit

By Rudy Martin

I went to work for IBM in Memphis in 1960.

Computers were just being invented.
Thousands of them were on order.

The most popular one was a 1401, and IBM had agreed to let us have one for three weeks.

Obviously, the salesmen in the branch wanted their prospects to see a demonstration tailored to their prospects—wholesale hardware companies, a chemical company, a savings and loan, a mortgage company, etc.

I was the only one in the branch that knew how to program (I had spent six weeks in St. Louis teaching customers how to program).

The salesman for financial-related companies was Clarence Banning. He was a great guy!

The talk of the town was a machine named a reader-sorter. It had thirteen pockets to put checks in so they could be distributed to the proper bank.

It read the little squiggly characters at the bottom of checks and put them in the proper pocket.

Clarence had some checks that he had "damaged." He would put them in his suit coat pocket and pull them out so he could demonstrate how the reader-sorter would put them in the reject pocket.

The demonstrations lasted three days, and before the last one started, I went to a pharmacy and bought a stuffed rabbit toy.

The meeting room was packed, and I was
standing behind the back row.

When he got to the part where he was going to demonstrate how the reader-sorter handled damaged checks, he reached into his vest to get a damaged check, and I reached into my vest and came out with the rabbit by its ears!

I thought that he was going to pass out!

He stuttered and stammered, then ended the demonstration!

Can't repeat what he said to me, but some canines were mentioned!

Rattlesnake

By Rudy Martin

I've been out and about in the great outdoors all
my life, but I've only seen one rattlesnake.

They're pretty rare in the delta of Arkansas,
where most of my activities have been.

Dad and I were fishing on Midway Lake when we saw what
looked like a beaver or some other animal swimming.

I started the motor, and we went to investigate.
We were startled to find it was a rattlesnake about five feet long.
He apparently was more buoyant than a water snake,
as most of his body was above the water.

He was cruising across the lake, at least two
hundred yards from the bank.
We always killed poisonous snakes, so we decided
that we didn't want him around.

Unfortunately, we didn't have the .22, so I
decided to kill him with a paddle.

I motored by him fast enough so that he couldn't
get us, and I swung at his body with a paddle.
After two or three passes, I managed to break
his back, and that really made him mad!

Unable to swim any longer, he opened his mouth
and struck at the paddle as I tried to kill him.

Finally I hit him in the head, and that finished him off.

We left him alone for a while, and then removed seven rattles.

Rex

By Rudy Martin

My dad got the first Labrador Retriever in Pine
Bluff, a male. He named him Shag.

A year later, a man got a female lab. They bred them, and
she had eight puppies—four black and four yellow.

The custom is the owner of the male gets the pick of the litter.

I picked a big yellow puppy and named him Rex.

Rex turned out to be a superb retriever—
whistle, hand signals, the works.

My dad leased a blind in the middle of 640 acres of green timber.

The hunting was superb.

One day, the ducks were landing way down at the
end of the clearing, so we moved down there.

I left Rex on his dog stand, and he wasn't a happy camper!

We were just getting settled when about
twenty mallards fell into the hole.

We killed several ducks, and when the smoke cleared,
I felt something pushing against my leg.

I looked down, and it was Rex sitting in the ice-cold water with
a drake mallard in his mouth! He was shivering like crazy!

I promptly went down and got his dog stand and
put it by a tree where we were standing.

He got an extra helping of canned red salmon that night!

Rex was also a clown. In the summertime, my mother would put one of those sprinklers that rotated back and front in the front yard.

Rex would straddle that sprinkler and let
that cool water cool him off!

Many times, my dad, my mother and I would sit on the front porch and laugh at his expression of "man this feels good!"

It wasn't unusual for cars driving by to pull over and point to him!

Ring, Ring, Ring

By Rudy Martin

This event happened when farmers still had to use wind-up phones.

A farmer had a cat that had gotten sick, so he wound up the phone and called the vet.

The vet thought that the farmer said that he had a sick calf, so he told him to give him a pint of castor oil!

The farmer said, "A pint of castor oil for a cat?" And the vet said, "Yes, it will clean him out good, and I'll be out at your place tomorrow."

The vet showed up the next day and asked about the sick calf, and the farmer said, "It's not a calf—it's a cat!"

The vet said, "Did he die?" And the farmer said, "No, he's out in the backyard with six other cats!"

"He's got two digging, two covering up, and two looking for new places!"

Rodey

By Rudy Martin

This saga started when my Uncle Son's cousin Ed Keith invited him to come from Pine Bluff to Magnolia to attend a Saturday night supper and barn dance in the country.

Son was in his early twenties, and the year was 1924.

When he arrived in Magnolia, he found out there was some trouble brewing.

Ed was the foreman at a sawmill, and there was some tension between the workers and management.

Ed relayed this to Son, but said it wouldn't involve him in any way.

He and Ed's mule Rodey made it to the supper and dance with no problems.

Ed had a steady girlfriend, so he left earlier than Son to pick up his date, taking a horse-pulled buggy.

Of course, the trip over was way before sunset, so he didn't give a thought to how different coming back would be.

He met several attractive girls at the supper and dance, even dancing with a couple of them.

The band was as he expected, complete with guitars, a fiddle, and a banjo.

The punch was spiked with whiskey made locally,
and he felt a little buzz after three cups of it.

Just before Son left, a couple of the workers at the sawmill
confronted Ed, creating some tense moments.

They told everybody in earshot that they were being
treated unfairly, and that things would have to change.

Ed admonished them to settle down, saying they would
discuss it further at the sawmill on Monday.

They walked away grumbling that this wasn't the end of it.

Son Martin told himself to relax, there was nothing to be afraid of.

Of course Son was on Rodey, returning to
Ed's house after the barn dance.

It was so dark he could barely make out Rodey's head
as they plodded down the unfamiliar dirt road.

The trip in had taken them about forty-five minutes,
and he guessed they were about halfway back.

There was no moon, and the trees covered the road anyway.

This was way before flashlights were invented,
and he had no kerosene lantern with him.

Wisely, he had loosened the reins to let Rodey lead the
way, confident that the mule would take them home.

Suddenly they were at the old wooden bridge they had
crossed in the daylight on the way to the dance.

As they started across, the clippety-clop of each of Rodey's steps echoed into the inky darkness, the sound fading into the abyss!

Trying to stay calm, he scolded himself silently, reasoning that the spooky sounds had nothing to do with his safety.

Then the image of Ichabod Crane and the Headless Horseman popped into his head, sending shivers down his spine!

"Just settle down, and we'll be there in a few minutes," he preached.

But when they reached the other side of the bridge, his worst fears were realized!

Someone reached out and grabbed Rodey's bridle and yelled, "Whoa!"

The mule tried to rear up when the unknown assailant grabbed his bridle, but the stranger had a firm grip. "Ed?" Came the question out of the darkness.

He tried to sound brave, but his response of, "No, this is Son Martin" sounded like it came from a soprano at the opera!

With that, the intruder let go of the bridle and slapped Rodey on his flank. The mule bolted down the invisible road at a full gallop.

Son was barely able to stay on by leaning down as close to Rodey's head as possible, hanging on for dear life.

Several branches hit him as they careened down the path, threatening to knock him off his only ticket home.

They arrived at Ed's house in a hurry, Rodey all lathered up and Son unable to breathe.

Rudy's Stories — 63

It wasn't until he had unsaddled the mule and wiped him down that he was finally able to take a deep breath.

His mind kept playing out various scenarios of what might have happened.

The rest of the night, he slept with one eye open. The *Legend of Sleepy Hollow* had nothing on him!

Rubbers

By Rudy Martin

A young man came into a drugstore. The druggist saw that he was acting nervous, so he went over to him and said, "Son, do you want to buy some rubbers?"

The young man said, "Yes sir," and the druggist said, "Come with me, I'll show you where they are."

When they got there, the druggist said, "It's none of my business, but do you have a hot date tonight?"

The young man said, "I don't know. I've never met her. She called me out of the blue and asked me if I'd like to have dinner tonight with her family!"

The druggist said, "Wow, I bet she's really hot. You'd better take two packages!"

So the young man bought two packages and left.

He rang the bell at the address she had given him, and her father answered the door.

They visited in the living room for a few minutes, then the mother said that dinner was ready.

When they got seated, the father asked the young man if he would ask the blessing, and he said, "Yes, sir."

Well, the young man went on and on and on and finally said, "Amen!'

His date leaned over and whispered in his ear, "I didn't know you were so religious." And the young man said, "I didn't know your father was a druggist!"

What a surprise!

Sam

By Rudy Martin

Rudy's black sambo was born in a chain link kennel.

As soon as he was grown, he could get out of everything!

He got out of the chain link kennel and the doghouse the four of us who were living in the "bachelor flat" had built!

We taught him to pick up his feeding pan when anyone came home.

One time, he got fed three times in one night!

George Falls came home first, fed him, and left.

Joe Pegram was next. He fed him and left.

I came home last, fed him, and left!

He could get out of a bowling ball, and he really seemed to enjoy escaping!

He disappeared for three weeks, and none of us thought we would ever see him again.

I ran an ad in the *Commercial Appeal* newspaper (Memphis's newspaper), and immediately a man called and said, "I've got your dog!"

All four of us jumped in the car and drove to the man's address. He had two young boys—one about ten and the other one about twelve. They had taught Sam to jump off the diving board!

He was in heaven!

Finally it was time to take him home, and the boys sobbed, trying to get us to leave him. Sometimes I regretted not leaving him.

I would let him in the bathroom when I was getting ready for work. I used Vitalis hair lotion, and when I used it, I let him sniff it.

He would go into a sneezing fit, sneezing and shaking his head! He would give me the dirtiest look imaginable!

One time, I put some shaving lather on a paw, and he limped!

He was by far the funniest dog I ever had!

Sam Got Mad at Me

By Rudy Martin

Three of us had had a good duck hunt in Government Cypress in Bayou Meto.

I have a johnboat with a 20 hp motor on it, and it goes pretty fast.

We were motoring along when all of a sudden, the lower unit hit a sunken log! Sam flew out of the boat into the water!

I immediately raised the lower unit out of the water so it wouldn't hit Sam, and he came up spitting and coughing!

He headed for the opposite bank!

Normally he lets me put him back in the boat by putting his front legs on the gunwale and me putting both hands on his neck so that he can arch his neck and pull himself into the boat.

But he wasn't having any of that—he was making a beeline for the opposite bank!

Of course, we were dying laughing!

When he got to the opposite bank, he got up on it, shook, and lay down!

I eased the bow of the boat up on the bank and gave him the command, "Kennel!" He didn't budge. I repeated the "kennel!" command, and he still didn't budge!

I carefully got out the boat, walked up to him, scratched his ears, and said, "I'm so sorry, Sam!"

The expression on his face was priceless! If dogs could talk, he was clearly saying, "So that's the thanks I get for fetching your ducks? Maybe I need to find a better boss!"

Sears

By Rudy Martin

When I was with IBM in Memphis, the branch manager would assign us trainees to go help customers who had requested help.

He assigned me to go help Sears.

One of the salesmen told me that Sears was replacing a Remington Rand computer and putting in an IBM computer, and the computer room was on the fourth floor.

As I was leaving, one of the salesmen pulled me aside and said that in the room before the computer room, there were about forty women working with Burroughs bookkeeping machines, and if I was alert, I could find one that was being "careless!"

Sure enough, I spotted one who was being "careless," and without looking where I was going, I walked into a big column!

It knocked me flat on my back, my briefcase skidded across the floor, and the whole room exploded with laughter!

Just for meanness, the branch manager sent me to Sears every time they called for help, and the room would buzz with, "That's the guy that walked into the column." "Really?" "Yeah, it knocked him flat on his back!"

Please don't send me back to Sears!

Shut It Off

By Rudy Martin

A man bought a Lincoln Navigator and stopped to fill it with gas. The owner left the engine running.

The attendant started filling the tank, and the pump ran and ran and ran.

The attendant tapped on the window and said, "Cap'n, would you mind shutting it off—you're gaining on me!"

Sigma Nu Relays

By Rudy Martin

The Sigma Nus put on what they call the
Sigma Nu relays each spring.

Instead of the men's fraternities competing,
it was the sorority girls who did.

They had ping-pong, badminton, horseshoes, touch football,
basketball competitions, and the most fun to watch was the tug-of-war, where the losing team got pulled through a muddy pond!

Now some of the guys had been drinking on the
last day—I said some—certainly not me!

We got "handsome and invisible" and decided to drive to
the Civil War Exhibit at Prairie Grove and pull one of the
cannons to Fayetteville and put it in the muddy pond!

We drove through the gate, backed up to a cannon, and guess
what? They didn't have 1 3/4" or 2" trailer balls back then!

I fished around in my car and came up with a
coat hanger, which we wound around the trailer
ball and part of the trailer for the cannon.

We got out of the park and headed for
Fayetteville with the cannon in tow.

It was pulling very well when all of a sudden, the
cannon passed us on the left side of the road!

It went about a hundred yards, did a column left, and crashed through a barbed wire fence!

We skedaddled back to Fayetteville!

We never heard anything about the rogue cannon, but we wondered if the farmer with it in his pasture wondered how in the hell that cannon got there!

Silver Chalices

By Rudy Martin

Growing up, my family went to Trinity Episcopal Church in Pine Bluff, Arkansas.

Reverend Ted Devlin was the man in charge there, and he told my dad that it was time for me to learn to be an acolyte.

Mr. Devlin trained me one Sunday after church, and I was surprised to learn that there is a lot for an acolyte to learn during communion.

Mr. Devlin was adamant that everything be done exactly right during communion.

For example, the wine cruet must always be in the left hand, and the water cruet must always be in the right hand.

He scheduled me to serve the next Sunday at 7:30 a.m.

My heart sank when I saw that the cruets were silver, not glass like they were when Mr. Devlin trained me!

When it was time for me to serve Mr. Devlin with the wine, I put it under my nose and took a strong sniff of it, and it was the wine!

Mr. Devlin looked startled but didn't say anything until the service was over.

Then he said, "Rudy, why in the world did you sniff the wine cruet?"

I said, "Because when you trained me, the cruets were clear, and today they are silver!"

Sneeze

By Rudy Martin

A man was going on an airplane trip. He found his seat and waited for the plane to take off.

Just before they closed the doors, this drop-dead gorgeous young woman sat down in the seat beside him.

They exchanged pleasantries, and the plane took off.

They had been airborne about fifteen minutes when the woman sneezed.

Just a few seconds later, the woman shuddered.

Another fifteen minutes later, the woman did the same thing—sneeze, shudder.

After the fourth sneeze, he said, "It's none of my business, but I've noticed that every time you sneeze, you shudder."

The woman looked around to be sure nobody could hear her and said, "I have a very rare condition." Sneeze, shudder. "The truth is that I have an orgasm after every sneeze!"

The man was taken aback and said, "My goodness, are you taking anything for it?" She said, "Yes, black pepper!"

So You Think I'm Frugal?

By Rudy Martin

To say that my dad was frugal would be the understatement of the century!

He lived out his stories of "he was so tight he wouldn't even spend the day" and "he was so tight he wouldn't even pay attention."

Of course, he lived through the Great Depression, so maybe his attitude about spending was understandable.

The bank furnished him a car, so we didn't get a family car until I was in the ninth grade.

That was in 1952, and the car was a 1936 Chevrolet.

My mother worked for a doctor, and she walked three blocks to the bus stop, rode the bus, then walked a block to the doctor's office.

We had a maid/cook who prepared a big noon meal, and my sister and I would come home from school, Mom would ride the bus, and Dad would come home from the bank for lunch.

Then we'd all reverse the process.

But he and Mom were able to put both my sister and I through college, an opportunity neither of them had.

When I got ready to go, my dad said, "Son, I want you to apply and enjoy yourself at college, but we need to have an understanding.

You'll meet lots of girls up there, and some of them will be looking for a husband.

If you walk down the aisle and say "I do," before I graduate, that means "I do quit school and go to work.""

Needless to say, I stayed single until I graduated!

And while I was in college, I had income from four sources: laundry/cleaning service for members of my fraternity, cigarette and candy machines in fraternity/sorority houses, sale of photos from fraternity/sorority parties, and booking bands for fraternity/sorority parties.

I almost had to take a pay cut when I went to work for IBM after I graduated!

Dad had an older 6HP outboard motor that never did run properly.

If he was hunting with us young folks, we got elected to crank that damn motor until we bloodied our knuckles.

This task would become his when he hunted with men his age.

One day, after a particularly frustrating session with this motor, Alwyn Dalrymple, a friend and practically a brother to me, and I offered to replace it with a brand-new 7 1/2HP motor free of charge to Dad.

Alwyn said, "Mr. Rufus, the next time you see this motor, it will be both a bigger and brand-spanking-new one, and it won't cost you a dime!"

Dad said, "I don't want a new motor. I like this one!"

Needless to say, the old motor stayed!

Later on, I was able to buy a 20HP motor with an electric start for myself, and it was a joy to use.

If Dad and I hunted together, we used it every time.

But if he hunted without me, it was back to me cranking on "Mr. Unreliable."

When I pressured him to use my motor, he said something might happen to it, and he would feel responsible.

I vividly remember saying "Dad, if you were to sink the whole boat and motor in the middle of the lake, never to be seen again, that would only represent a small fraction of the value of your things I broke or lost when I was growing up."

But my words fell on deaf ears.

Finally, one year, the farm we own made a nice profit, and I traded the cranky old motor for a year-old 9.8HP Mercury motor with an electric start.

I didn't ask for permission because I knew what his answer would be.

We had just arrived at the lake (in separate cars) when I told him I had a present for him in the back of my station wagon.

His eyes got really big when he saw it, and I had to endure the expected objections!

But he ended up loving it, and even left it on a boat at a reservoir where during the spring and summer, he and a friend his age fished once a week.

Before that, the two seventy-plus-year-olds would
haul Mr. Unreliable back and forth each trip.

It really felt good to me to see him go first class for a change!

It's ironic to me that my friends and family all think
that I'm frugal—prone to use things that are old.

They're also convinced I'm a board-certified pack rat.

But compared to Dad, I'm a spendthrift!

It's fascinating now to reflect on the unspoken arrangement
we had when we worked on the duck blinds on Pipkin Lake
on the farm we bought after I started working for IBM.

One blind was Dad's favorite (the point blind),
and one was my favorite (the island blind).

Without ever discussing it, over the years, we reached
an agreement to let the person whose favorite blind
was being worked on call all the shots!

If we were working on his blind and we needed a 10' 2 × 4,
he would make do by scabbing two 6' boards together!

If we needed the same board on my blind, nothing would
do but to drop everything and head to town to buy one!

It's amazing that a simple two-minute boat ride from one blind
to the other would completely flip-flop the pecking order!

He even laughingly said that my friend Tabby Benton
and I were part of the "throwaway generation"—if
it's broken, throw it away and buy a new one.

One year, the ice on the lake tangled the decoy lines into big balls.
He took them home and spent hour upon
hour getting them straightened out.

He and my mother almost got a divorce because
he was untangling those damn strings!

A friend offered to furnish all new line for the decoys so we
could start fresh, but he wouldn't have any part of it!

"There's nothing wrong with this line that a
little work won't solve," he snorted.

I have to admit that as I've grown older, I'm getting more
like him every day, and I catch a lot of flak from my kids
and hunting partners about patching up something with
friction tape and baling wire instead of buying a new one.

I guarantee you that nobody I know can hold a candle
to me when it comes to untangling a decoy line!

And no, we don't need new line!

Dad, I miss you!

I loved you with every bone in my body!

I can't wait to join you in heaven!

Spilled Dog Food

By Rudy Martin

Growing up, we had two Labrador Retrievers—Shag and Rex.

We had a wire kennel for them, but in the summertime, it was too hot, so we let them roam free.

They liked to get between the nandina bushes and the house and lie on the cool dirt.

You couldn't see them when they were there.

We used dog food from Bobo Seed and Feed, and Dad had ordered some.

I was sitting on the screened-in back porch when I heard a man yelling, "Help, Help!"

I spied a young man about ten feet up a small tree, obviously terrified!

I ran out of the screened-in porch and saw what was happening.

Rex and Shag were lying on the cool dirt behind the nandina bushes and heard the young man whistling.

They wouldn't hurt a fly, but he didn't know that.

They burst out of the bushes barking loudly, and that's when the man climbed the tree.

He had come from the company pickup carrying a twenty-five-pound bag of dog food on each shoulder, and he dropped both of them when the commotion started. Both bags split open, so the dogs had a feast!

After he calmed down, he told me that was the scariest thing that had ever happened to him!

Spotlight in Our Eyes

By Rudy Martin

Bill Tedford and I did a whole lot of hunting, fishing, and frog gigging while we were at the U of A in Fayetteville.

It was the opening day of dove season, and we had seen some doves around a small pond outside of Springdale. We didn't see any no trespassing signs around it, so we assumed it wasn't posted.

As I walked around the pond, several big bull frogs jumped into the water. We decided to come back and gig there that night.

You should have seen the red eyes that shone around the pond when we arrived!

We were taking turns and putting our frogs on a fish stringer.

We had made it around about halfway around the pond when this spotlight came on, blinding both of us!

Then we saw the business end of a gun barrel pointing right at us!

It looked like it was a foot around!

Then a voice from the darkness said, "What are you boys doing?"

I immediately raised the stringer of frogs and replied, "Gigging frogs!"

A man turned the spotlight off and said, "You boys are mighty lucky. I almost shot you!"

It turned out that someone had stolen one of his calves, and when he saw our light going across his pasture, he assumed that it was that man coming to steal another calf!

We offered him some or all the frogs we had, but he let us keep them.

He even said we could come again if we let him know ahead of time.

Quickies

By Rudy Martin

- What did the Indian say to the mermaid? "How?"

- What did the skunk say when the wind changed? "It all comes back to me now!"

- Three Martians landed their spaceship in the states. They were really short—about three feet tall. One of them was looking around and came upon Wonder Woman!

- He took one look at her and said, "Take me to your ladder. I'll see your leader later!"

- A man ran into a bar and yelled at the bartender, "Quick, quick, quick! How big does a penguin get?" The bartender said, "Oh, about knee high." The man said, "Oh my god! Call an ambulance. I ran over a nun!"

- Two men were sitting in a bar when a good-looking woman walked by them wearing a spandex outfit and no panties. One of them said, "Did you see that?" The other one said, "Yeah, it looked like two pigs fighting in a Kroger Sack!"

21 Shots

By Rudy Martin

I hunted a lot with Tommy Stobaugh in Bayou Meto.

He was the best wing shot I ever hunted with.

Many times, I've seen him kill three drakes
when a drove came over treetop high.

One Saturday, seven of us were hunting together,
and at nine, we hadn't popped a cap.

We were all sitting on a big tree that had
fallen, all lined up like ducks in a row.

The only food we had was I had a king-size Snickers
in my pocket, and when I got it out, it felt like
six sets of eyes were drooling over it.

All of a sudden, Tommy shushed us and nodded
that something was coming from his left.

It was a drake mallard flying solo!

Seven of us called at him, and he immediately
cupped his wings and started right towards us.

Tommy whispered, "I'll tell you when." And he yelled, "Now"
when he was maybe twenty yards from us and below the timber.

Nobody cut a feather!

The only damage anyone saw was that he made it off with both wings over his ears!

He did make a high pass back over us, and we all saw him giving us the finger!

We made Mr. Winchester happy that day!

By the Antlers

By Rudy Martin

Two Texas Aggies were deer hunting and killed a nice buck.

They were dragging it through the brush by its hind legs.

They passed another hunter, and he said, "Guys, you need to tie a rope around its antlers. That way, its legs will fold back under, making it much easier to drag through the brush.

The Aggies thanked the man and did as he said.

After a few minutes, one of the Aggies said, "The man was right—this is much easier, but we're getting farther from the pickup!"

Bubba

By Rudy Martin

He was Son Martin to his friends and to the
community, but to us he was Bubba!

For as long as I can remember, the extended family of
the Martin clan has always been close, and we still have a
happening every year during the Christmas holidays!

A few years older than Dad, Bubba was
extremely liked by all who knew him.

When I was growing up, he owned a dry cleaning business, and
I picked up and delivered dry cleaning for a couple of years.

Later, he closed the business and went to work for the
Employment Security Division, where he matched men
available as laborers in the community with people
who needed a laborer for one or more days.

His two children were both daughters, so I became his surrogate son!

We spent many hours fishing and hunting
together, and he taught me a lot!

He also loved to sing and was a member of a barbershop
quartet that won a big contest singing "Kentucky Babe!"

When I became a member of a barbershop quartet, he loved
it when we practiced at his and my aunt Frances's house!

And speaking of her, she was always Aunty Panty to the Martin clan!

It seems that one of her nieces came up with that, and it stuck!

Undoubtedly the trait I most admired about him was his positive mental attitude.

I was in awe of him and somewhat envious of this trait. It made me love him even more!

Whatever activity we were engaged in was "Top Drawer!"

A simple breakfast I fixed would elicit, "That's the finest breakfast I've ever had."

Even a mediocre duck hunt would produce "That's the best duck hunt I've ever been on."

I clearly remember going over to their house on special occasions in the summer. He would serve charcoal steak cooked on the stone cooker in the summer. I still use his special barbeque sauce on several kinds of meat, especially duck.

Bubba, I will always love you!

I was honored to be a pallbearer at Bubba's funeral!

Bambi

By Rudy Martin

When I was a senior in college at the U of A, the starting halfbacks for the Razorbacks were Jim Mooty and Lance Alworth.

Both were all American that year!

Alworth was a high draft pick of the San Diego Chargers.

He made all-pro every year he played!

Bananas

By Rudy Martin

When I was growing up, every drugstore had a soda fountain.

One afternoon, a little boy about seven years old came in the store and sat down at the counter.

He was dressed just like a cowboy—cowboy boots, double pistols, chaps, and a ten-gallon hat!

The waitress came up to him and said, "Hi, Tex, what can I do for you?"

The boy drew both of his pistols and said, "I tell you what you can do, you can fix me a banana split!

I want a scoop of chocolate, one of vanilla and one of strawberry," and put his pistols back in their holsters!

The waitress said, "Okay, Tex. Settle down. I'll fix it just like you want it!"

The waitress busied herself putting it together. She said, "You want crushed nuts?"

The boy drew both of his pistols and said, "You want your boobies shot off?"

The waitress fainted!

Bass Around Our Feet

By Rudy Martin

In college, my roommate was Bill Tedford, and we loved to hunt and fish around Fayetteville, Arkansas. We found a small pond one afternoon, and to our surprise, it was full of bass! I had a fly rod, and he had a Zebco reel on a casting rod!

We were standing at the edge of the water!

The bass were hitting anything we threw, so we soon had a bunch of bass flopping around our feet!

Out of nowhere, a truck appeared, and a man started cussing us, saying we were on his posted land, and we'd better leave right now or he would call the sheriff!

We ran to Bill's jeep and drove away in a cloud of dust, leaving the bass in the tall grass!

Battery

By Rudy Martin

Henry Trotter Jr. had enough money to buy every battery in Arkansas, but wouldn't buy one and instead took one out of a car or truck on the Trotter Fork Parking Lot.

I was terrified that a cop would catch us stealing one and a spotlight would be shining in our faces!

We never got caught, but I was always scared we would be.

Beaver Hutt

By Rudy Martin

David Ziegler, from Tallahassee, Florida came to Arkansas to duck hunt with me several times.

It was a bitter cold day, and we were laying on a beaver hut.

Ducks were everywhere! We quickly quit shooting anything but mallards, and there were plenty of them!

David had laid his glove on the beaver hut, and when he tried to put it on, it was frozen solid to the beaver hut!

He did have a hand warmer, and that helped some.

We finished our limit in about an hour and retreated to my clubhouse for a hot toddy!

We got tiddly!

That afternoon he saw me triple on snow geese in a rice field!

I had my dog Jake with me.

The first two shot dropped in the decoys, but the third one set his wings and landed in a bean field about two hundred yards away! Jake had him marked, but the goose tried to take off when Jake got to him!

The chase was on!

Jake finally caught him by the butt but not
until after a seventy-five-yard chase!

He was one-proud puppy when he brought him in!

Later David brought me a Notarized
Affidavit that witnessed everything!

Bennett's Reservoir

By Rudy Martin

In high school, Henry Trotter, Andy Payne, and I duck hunted on Bennett's reservoir near Stuttgart. Andy's dad, Dr. Virgil Payne, leased a blind there for us.

It was a huge blind that faced the wrong way, so shooting opportunities were scarce—maybe a coot or water turkey.

There was a floating blind about three hundred yards south of us, and they killed quite a few ducks. We called it "the floater."

It was nine o'clock on Saturday morning, and we hadn't popped a cap.

All of a sudden, "the floater" fired a volley of shots. We saw several ducks fall in their decoys, but one duck cupped his wings and headed straight for us! It was a drake mallard!

We whispered for everybody to be still, and just as he got into our range, he folded dead just outside of our decoys!

Of course, we whooped and hollered that that was our duck, and they yelled back, "You sons of bitches, get in your boat and bring us our duck!"

We got in our boat, picked up the duck, and headed toward their blind.

We stopped just short of their decoys, held up the duck, and yelled, "Na-na-na-na-na-na, na-na-na-na-na-na," then all of us gave them the finger!

We never told Dr. Payne!

Ann Setzer

By Rudy Martin

I met Ann Setzer at a cocktail party in Memphis.

She was beautiful—Miss Memphis of 1956—and we started dating and quickly fell in love.

She had a beautiful voice and got to sing in Fred Waring's choir at a concert.

She had choir practice in her church on Monday night.

I was the only one watching/listening to it.

A woman was standing up holding her baby in the choir.

He/she became fretful and the woman asked me if I would watch her baby until choir practice was over.

Are you talking to me?

The baby was content for a while, and then started squalling!

Ann said my face turned bright red!

We were deeply in love, but I really messed up for not asking Ann to marry me!

The last I heard someone told me that she was moving to Louisville, Kentucky.

Close but no cigar!

Can Sam Go Huntin'?

By Rudy Martin

Mr. Joe Hickerson was a farmer friend of Dad's, and he lived south of Altheimer on the bank of Swan Lake. He was a soft-spoken man with a slow, deliberate talking style.

He owned some prime green timber property, and one year soon after I had moved back to Pine Bluff, he invited Dad and I to come down for a duck hunt. The water where the ducks were using was shallow—just over our ankles.

Mr. Joe had never hunted with a retriever, but he graciously invited me to bring my lab, Sam (Rudy's Black Sambo). Sam was a very, very good retriever, obedient, whistle/hand-signal trained, super nose—the complete package.

Ducks were everywhere, and Sam had a field day running through the shallow water!

Mr. Joe was in awe of Sam's performance and couldn't get over how Sam would move to where he could see me, then sit in the cold water when I blew my whistle! Often trees would block his line of sight, and he would peer around them to find me. Then with a hand signal, he was off to find the duck!

Sam selected an area by a big fallen tree to pile up the ducks!

Mr. Joe shot a drake mallard, and Sam brought it back to the designated drop-off point!

The duck was still alive, so of course, he climbed off the pile of ducks into the water every time Sam let him go!

Sam retrieved him several times while we watched with great amusement!

He was real soft mouthed, so he wasn't hurting the duck at all!

After about the fifth retrieve, Sam uttered a deep growl while holding the duck in his mouth!

He was obviously saying, "I'm really getting tired of this you SOB. If you climb off this pile one more time, I'm going to punch your lights out!"

I finally relented and put the drake out of its misery!

About Wednesday of the next week, Mr. Joe called my dad and said, "I want to invite Sam to go hunting with me Saturday, and if you and little Rudy can't come, could you put Sam on the bus and let me get him off at Cornerstone!"

A Tribute to My Dad

By Rudy Martin

My dad and I had a very special father-son relationship. We were different in a lot of ways, but we loved each other deeply and respected the other's point of view. I often wish I could talk to him now and ask his opinion about something that's bothering me.

It's 2002 now, and a lot has happened in my life since he left us! First and foremost, I've allowed God to come into my life! After years of being passive in my religious beliefs, I've come to realize that only He can provide the peace and serenity we all seek! I've got a long way to go spiritually, but at least I've started my journey!

My kids are young adults now, and two of the three are married. Last fall, I even became the grandfather of a precious little girl! And I've found a wonderful woman to share my life with who loves me and patiently puts up with my habits and idiosyncrasies!

At sixty-three years of age, my skills on the tennis court have diminished, but I'm convinced that I'm a better wing shot than I've ever been! I can still chunk a floating plug right next to a cypress knee and flip a popping bug where I want it to go!

Dad never had a cushy life. He dropped out of high school in the eleventh grade. His father had died, and he needed to take care of his mother. They lived in a big house at twenty-fourth and olive, where they had boarders.

In spite of his lack of a formal education, he was very knowledgeable about an amazing number of subjects. He was a voracious reader, and he used TV programs to increase his knowledge about a variety of things. I remember being in awe of his penmanship, which had a beautiful, flowing style.

He started out sweeping the floors for Citizen's Bank in Pine Bluff. That was in about 1920. When that bank closed during the depression, he joined Simmons Bank. During his tenure there, he worked as a bookkeeper, a teller, vice president, cashier, and finally senior vice president and chief agricultural officer. At one stage, the bank sent him to manage a farm in Bastrop, Louisiana, to protect a loan the bank had made.

He was elected to the board of directors of Simmons Bank and served on it for many years. In all he was at Simmons for forty-seven years, retiring when he was sixty-five (a mandatory requirement of the bank). I deem it quite remarkable that he was able to rise to the title of senior vice president, a tribute to his desire and work ethic.

After he retired from the bank, he went into the real estate business, passing the broker's exam on the first attempt! He was president of a local real estate firm for several years, and he often would lament that he made more money in his first year in the real estate business than he did in his forty-seventh year at the bank!

Early on, he worked out of his home, and he was considering a slogan for the business, which was named Rudy's Corner!

Apparently a real estate broker has to have a sign advertising his business, so Dad was pondering what to put on the end of the carport. He came up with what he thought was a wonderful slogan—Get A Lot While You're Young!

Normally my mother stayed in the background, letting Dad pretty much run the show,
But this time, she said in no uncertain terms that those words would not be on their carport!

Probably the trait most people remember about him is that he always had a joke for them.

People would come into the bank (for business or just to see him), and they would always leave laughing.

His repertoire of jokes was phenomenal—a subject would trigger a punch line!

Jim Ed Brown, a Country and Western singer from Pine Bluff who made it big in Nashville, would come by the bank occasionally to see Dad.

> Jim Ed would encourage him to pursue a career as an after-dinner speaker after he retired from the bank.

When he did retire from the bank Jim Ed even put him in contact with his agent in Nashville, and for several years, Dad and Mom traveled all over the south, where he was the featured speaker!

> He called himself the Serious Humorist!

His style was to make a number of serious points, illustrating each one with a humorous story!

> Often he would find out the name of a bald-headed man in the audience before the banquet started, and he would open his talk with, "I'm going to tell you some stories tonight—some may even make your hair fall out—but I see that old Bob Jones (the bald-headed man) has already heard them!"

The main theme he used was, "Let's Look In The Mirror," where he encouraged his audience to take responsibility for their own actions and not blame things on the other fellow: "This fellow comes into the Psychiatrist's office with a fried egg sitting on top of his head and a strip of bacon hanging down over each eye! He looks at the shrink and says, 'Doc, I need to talk to you about my brother!'"

I still have several of his brochures!

I wrote this when I was sixty-three, and I'm now eighty-four and in my twilight years! I've lived a full life, and I can't wait to reunite with all of my family in heaven!

Dad, I miss you!

Thank you and Mom for starting me off right!

I loved y'all with every bone in my body!

I can't wait to join you in heaven!

Little Rudy

Donald Dell and Chuck McKinley

By Rudy Martin

When I was a senior in college, I dated a cute redheaded girl named Paula from Tulsa.

She had told me that her dad owned the largest shopping center in the United States.

She had invited me to spend the weekend with her and her parents.

As we pulled into her parents' driveway, I noticed that the Tulsa Tennis Club was right across from them.

When I pulled into their driveway, I was greeted by a Lamborghini, a Jaguar, and a Rolls-Royce!

I knew right then I was in way, way over my head!

She introduced me to her parents, and they were very nice.

Her dad said, "I understand that you play tennis."

I said, "Yes, sir, I do. I lettered three years for the Razorbacks."

He said, "That's great, I entered you in the tournament!"

"Six of the top 10 players in the US will be here—it starts tomorrow at 9:00 a.m."

We walked across the street to look at the draw, and I'm scheduled to play the number 6 player in the country—Donald Dell of Yale University!

We would play the opening match in the 1960 Tulsa Invitational at 9:00 a.m. tomorrow!

I figured that if we start at 9:00, we'd be finished by 9:15!

Paula's dad and I walked across the street Saturday morning around 8:15.

At 8:30, the umpire called for the players scheduled to play at 9:00 report to court 1.

It's customary for the players to get a five-minute warm-up before starting to play.

I did miserably in the warm-up. Sometimes I didn't even make contact with the ball!

The umpire said, "Ladies and gentlemen, welcome to the Tulsa Invitational tournament. In the north court, I have the number 6 player in the US—Mr. Donald Dell!"

"And in the south court, I have Mr. Rudy Martin, a member of the University of Arkansas tennis team."

The umpire called us to the net. I won the toss and elected to serve.

We took our practice serves, and the umpire said, "Ball boys ready, linesmen ready, players ready, play!"

I always bounce the ball on the court once before I serve. I did that, and the ball hit right on the toe of my shoe and dribbled onto the court!

The crowd and Donald Dell roared!

I hit four of my best serves, each one in a corner of the Service Court, and I never touched the ball—he hit four winners!

When we changed courts at 0–1, I said to Don, "Mr. Dell, if you do that again, I'm going to have to kick you in the knee!"

He beat me 6–0, 6–3 and could have easily beaten me 6–0, 6–0, but I think he was getting used to the court, the wind, the bounce of the ball, the sun, etc.

So there you have it—a country boy from Pine Bluff, Arkansas played the number 6 player in the United States!

A Little Bitty Toad Frog

By Rudy Martin

My roommate, Bill Tedford, and I were the Mark Twain's of the SAE house at the U of A in Fayetteville.

Anything that swam, flew, ran, jumped, or crawled was fair game to us.

We especially loved to catch frogs at night with our hands! They were delicious fried!

One night, an SAE brother asked if he could go with us, and we agreed. His name was Don Smith.

On the way, we told Don that since we would be catching them with our hands, we had to be extra careful that a cottonmouth moccasin was nowhere to be found!

He chastised us severely about being afraid
of snakes, even called us sissies!

That night we were taking turns, and Don was up to bat!

The spotlight shone on a huge bullfrog,
and Don knelt down to grab it!

He was inches away when a tiny, little bitty toad
frog jumped and landed on his hand!

Don let out a yell and fell down trying to get away!

Of course we were yelling, "Snake, snake!"

I can't repeat what he said to me, but some canines were mentioned!

You mean that you were afraid of a tiny,
little bitty, pissant toad frog?

An SOB in Manitoba

By Rudy Martin

Ed Apple, a friend of mine, and I drove to Manitoba, Canada, to hunt Canada geese. He brought his field trial lab. We were to meet four men from Iowa who were supposedly experienced goose hunters.

We introduced ourselves, and a man named Randy didn't give us eye contact or shake our hands. Ed looked at me and said, "Oh brother, this guy is a genuine SOB, and we're going to have to put up with him the whole trip." Truer words were never spoken.

At supper, he dominated the talking, and smoke came out of Ed's ears when Randy told him to shut up.

I pulled one of the other men in their party and said, "What's the scoop on this yo-yo?"

He said that Randy:

made all the arrangements,
insisted that he be the lead car all the way from Iowa,
had decided that we would not have guides without asking us,
told horribly dirty jokes that weren't funny, and
had a female lab that was poorly trained.

At breakfast the next morning, his lab was eating my breakfast. I yelled at her and slapped her on the nose, and Randy went ballistic! He yelled, "You SOB, don't you ever touch my dog again or I'll beat your ass to a pulp." I didn't want to get into a fight, so I let it go. He never spoke to me again, which was "Jim Dandy" with me!

They had gotten there the previous morning, but they didn't do any scouting. We decided to join Randy's group that morning. We all struck out following Randy, and he got lost twice driving by fields we'd been by before. He finally announced that we were going to hunt a canola field and didn't fire a shot until some of Randy's group found a pond that ducks were using.

Shots were fired, and we heard Randy screaming at his lab.

Ed and I walked over to the pond with his dog, and we walked up to the pond's edge and spied six dead ducks anywhere from thirty to a hundred yards from where we were.

Randy was screaming at his lab and throwing clods of mud toward the ducks. She just walked away and lay down.

Ed heeled his field trial lab to the edge of the water and sent him on six blind retrieves with a minimum of direction.

Randy threw his lab in the bed of his pickup and roared off in a cloud of dust.

When we finished lunch, Ed and I decided to scout on our own. The hell with Randy!

We were about thirty miles from the town we were staying in and Ed was taking a nap when I spotted about three hundred Canada geese feeding in a wheat field. I woke Ed up, and I drove by the field again so Ed could see.

Neither of us will trespass on posted land, so we drove around and found a house about a mile from the geese.

Ed knocked on the door, and I heard him say, "Could you tell me how to get to St. Louis?" A woman said, "Did you say St. Louis?" And he said, "Yes, ma'am."

At first, she thought he was serious, then he told her about the geese. She said if we would drive her by them, she should be able to tell us who owned that property. We did, and she said that the land belonged to the Mennonites, and she showed us where their headquarters were.

We drove her back to her house, and she laughed and said, "Anytime you guys need directions to St. Louis, stop by the house and I'll direct you."

We drove into the Mennonites' headquarters, and a man stopped us and asked us if he could help us.

We told him about the geese on their land, and he said he had seen them, and he would have to ask the Mennonites' leader if we could hunt there.

He came back in a few minutes and said we could hunt there, but for us to be careful around the sheep.

We were super excited when we drove back to the motel.

Then Randy showed up and told us his party would be going with us the next day.

The field we were going to hunt in the morning was big—around 350 acres. Two of the men with Randy hunted with us. When we arrived there, I set up our spread where the geese had been yesterday, while Ed showed Randy where they needed to set up at the opposite end of the field.

Our group ended up with fourteen Canadas and would have had more if Randy's group hadn't been shooting at geese that were too high, and they wouldn't stay still. Randy said that their group would have done better if we had set them up in a better place.

Rudy's Stories — 115

After our last hunt, Randy had the gall to announce that next year his group would be coming to Arkansas to hunt on our land.

We said not *no* but *Hell No*. And that was the last we ever saw of Randy.

A No-Win Situation

By Rudy Martin

During the height of the war in Ireland between the Catholics and the Protestants, a man was walking down a street with no streetlights.

As he passed a dark alley, a man ran out of the alley, put a knife to the man's throat, and said, "Identify yourself!"

The man said to himself, "I'm screwed. If I say I'm a Catholic and he's a Protestant, I'm a goner, and if say I'm a Protestant and he's a Catholic, I'm a goner. I've had it!"

He thought about it for a minute and said, "I'm Jewish!"

The man with the knife said, "I must be the luckiest Arab in Ireland!"

A Spill in Stillwell

By Rudy Martin

My senior year at the U of A, I dated a very cute girl
from Stillwell, Oklahoma, Donna Carson.

She was a medium height blonde with curves in all the right places.

We had a lot of fun together. She invited me to
stay with her and her parents for a few days.

The second day, her dad took us water skiing
on a lake that was close to Stillwell.

I let Donna ski first, and she did just fine.

When it was my time, I put their slalom
ski in the water and used it.

I'm no expert, but I'm pretty damn good if I do say so myself.

I love to get on one side of the boat, really
lean toward it, and jump both waves!

Mr. Carson made a wide, sweeping turn, and I saw my
chance at popping the whip unfold before my eyes!

I was on the left side of the boat, and he was turning
left, so I bent my knees and jumped both waves!

Unfortunately, at the height of my jump, the rope broke!

Donna said I went tumbling end over
end, completely out of control!

My front foot came out of the slalom, and my back foot
hit it, knocking a pretty good chunk out of my big toe.

Mr. Carson had a first aid kit, and he patched me up.

Needless to say, my skiing was over for the day!

I was a year ahead of her in school. I was working for
IBM in Memphis, and Donna came to visit me for a
weekend. She stayed with a good friend of hers.

I gave her the two-bit tour of Memphis and
took her to three nice restaurants.

We kissed goodbye, with promises that we would meet again soon.

She went to work for Foley's department store in Houston.

I enlisted in the Air National Guard in Memphis to keep from
getting drafted, and I spent eight weeks of Basic Training
at Lackland Air Force Base in San Antonio, Texas.

I called her, and she agreed to come visit
me when I had some leave time.

She got us a room, and we made hay while the sun was shining!

We talked on the phone a few times when I got back to Memphis, but things tapered off, and I fell in love with Miss Memphis of 1955.

I have many fond memories of my times with Donna.

She is truly a classy lady!

A Summer Vacation

By Rudy Martin

Paula was thirteen, and she had told him that she was sixteen.

I took Paula into a back room and said, "Paula, you are not about to go out with a boy who is nineteen."

She fussed for a minute, then said, "Okay."

The girls had a ball on the beach, but I had to put my foot down when Josh asked Paula to go into the bedroom with him!

I took Paula into a back room and said, "Paula, you are not about to go out with a boy who is nineteen!"

She fussed for a minute then said, "Okay."

I said not *no*, but *hell no!*

Talk about naive!

Wrong Way

By Rudy Martin

Back in the sixties, there was an all-pro tackle who played for the Los Angeles Rams. His name was Jim Marshall, and he was a terror on the field!

The score was tied with thirty seconds to play when the opposing quarterback fumbled the ball!

Jim Marshall saw the loose ball, scooped it up, and ran ninety yards in the wrong direction!

He was tackled in the opposing team's end zone, giving them two points as time ran out!

Wousy

By Rudy Martin

This man had a blind date with a woman.

He picked her up at her house, and she was a good-looking woman.

He took her to the carnival.

They rode a few rides, and he asked her what she wanted to do next.

She said, "I want to get weighed."

So he took her to the man who guesses weights, and he weighed her.

He asked her what she wanted to do next, and
She said, "I want to get weighed."

After they did that the third time, he got
frustrated and took her home.

Her mother said, "Honey, did you have a good time?"

She said, "Wousy!"

Who Me?

By Rudy Martin

The lady's voice on the line delivered the message I
had expected but somehow hoped I wouldn't get!

He had been run over on Cantrell Road!

Jake had been gone for four days, but I was
clinging to the hope that he was okay.

I thanked her for the message and arranged for them
to keep him in a freezer until I could make plans
To pick him up and bury him on my farm.

Jake was one of eleven lab puppies.

His momma and daddy were both black, and
he was the only puppy that wasn't.

He was technically a
chocolate, but his fur was almost red, much
lighter than a typical chocolate.

I had never owned a chocolate, so of course I had to keep him!

Suzie died shortly after Jake was born, but he kept the
bloodline going. His daddy's name was Jake, so I thought
it appropriate to name him Jake's Chocolate Rebel!

They were out of Super Chief, one of the all-time great retrievers!

I had a blast watching them go from furry
little balls to feisty puppies!

By the time I let people get them (at seven weeks), I had
them trained to stop barking if they got too loud!

They would hightail it for their doghouse if I spoke sharply to them!

People were amazed that they would mind me at that young age!

My fiancée, Mary Jane Melton, basically wanted
a housedog, and we could tell by the size of Jake's
feet that he was going to be too big!

I lived across the street from my fiancée until we
married, so Jake was with his momma and me!

His ears flopped all over the place, meaning of course
that he would have finished last at a dog show!

I had his part of the backyard graveled, and he would
pick up a rock if he couldn't find anything else!

He loved leaning against your legs, reveling in
the feeling of his body against yours!

He weighed eighty-two pounds, but he
was way more lover than fighter!

For some reason, I didn't spend much time training Jake initially.

He was a natural sight retriever, and I was
content with that for his first three years.

With a sack of rocks, I could show him where I wanted him to go.

Then when he was three, I admonished myself for
being lazy, and we began training in earnest.

He picked it up very quickly and soon was
on a par with Kate, his momma.

The main place I duck hunt is Pipkin Lake,
outside Pine Bluff, Arkansas.

The dog platform is attached to the blind, separated by a wall.

The space where Jake sat is open in the front,
with wire on the side, back, and overhead.

When the wire was brushed, he was pretty much invisible.

A ladder attached to the platform provided a way for
him to climb back on when returning with a duck.

If things got slow, I'd let Jake come into the blind, and he would
immediately start picking up the ducks he had already retrieved!

Of course, this was a ploy to get attention,
complete with the obligatory ear rub.

And you'd better watch your sausage biscuit or
doughnut—it could disappear in a flash!

We had around two hundred duck decoys around this blind, and
he quickly learned to tell the difference between duck and decoy.

He would mark the ducks as they fell and would obey
my commands to fetch them in the order I wanted.

If we crippled a duck, the chase was on!

All ducks dive under the water when pursued, but diving ducks (scaup, ringnecks, redheads, etc.) are masters at it.

Jake would start swimming in circles when the duck would dive, then make a beeline for it when it surfaced!

Sometimes this would go on for several minutes, with him getting farther and farther from the blind!

The longest retrieve I ever saw (in terms of time) was several years ago on another lake.

My party had finished its hunt, and we were standing by our vehicles.

My friend Alf Williams had hunted in the other party, and he said that they had a dead mallard drake that the wind had blown to the bank.

I asked Alf if it was okay if Jake fetched it, and he said sure.

Sure enough, I could see a drake mallard on its back floating against the bank.

When Jake got close to the duck, it flipped over and started swimming away!

The chase was on!

The drake kept diving and reappearing, with Jake in hot pursuit!

Jake would get to within inches of the drake, only to have him dive again!

Of course, he and I had a peanut gallery by this time, and everyone was cheering him on!

Finally, Jake managed to stick his head underwater and grab the drake by the butt!

Nobody ever looked at their watch, but everyone agreed later that at least thirty minutes elapsed!

I was one proud parent when he turned wearily for home!

His triumphant return was complete with high fives all around and a standing ovation!

If a dog could talk, when his feet finally hit the bottom, the expression on his face said, "A dead duck, huh? Right!"

I don't think he ever forgave Alf!

When he was about ten months old (his first duck season), he got hypothermia!

The temperature was down in the teens, and we had waded in waist-deep water for about fifteen minutes.

All of a sudden, he climbed onto a fallen tree and wouldn't budge!

I went over to him, and he was shaking all over!

I knew he was in big trouble, so I got one of the guys to carry my gun while I carried him out of the woods!

Fortunately, I had a towel back at the boat, and I rubbed him vigorously with it for a few minutes, fluffing his fur the wrong way!

Soon he was as lively as ever!

Needless to say, that ended his hunting for the day!

Once my fiancée and I got stranded in a blind
and had to spend the night there.

Amazingly she married me anyway!

Carelessly I let the boat float away!

During the night, it got down below freezing, and she put him
across her lap and used his body heat to keep her warm!

Of course, he loved the attention!

Jake loved it when we stayed in my travel
trailer on the bank of Pipkin Lake.

By this time, I had his brother Cheech (same
mother and father—different litters)!

Cheech was a beautiful black lab, but he
was a few bricks shy of a load!

If I was brushing the blind or putting out decoys
before the season, they would often run around
the bank to keep as close to me as possible.

They even swam out to the blind and back several times!

At night, I would let them come inside the trailer, and
they would snooze on the floor beside my bed.

Later we rented a clubhouse, and they enjoyed
socializing with the other hunters and dogs there!

I was hunting in one end of a rice field, and a friend
from Florida was hunting in the other.

About forty snow geese flew low over the
field, way out in front of me.

Suddenly they turned and flew directly over my
head, no more than thirty yards high.

The first two dropped in my decoys, but the third one set his wings and landed in a bean field about two hundred yards away! Jake had him marked, and the goose tried to take off when Jake got to him!

Jake locked in on him while he was in
the air and took off in a sprint!

The goose started running, but he was no
match for Jake on the dry ground!

My friend whooped from the other end of the field and later even sent me a notarized affidavit stating that he saw the whole thing!

He lived to be twelve, and I stopped taking
him hunting when he was ten.

His spirit was willing, but physically he just couldn't do it anymore.

I was not about to ask him to do more
than he was capable of doing.

I still took him to the clubhouse for the weekend, but his retrieving was relegated to fetching sticks in the yard for the young boys.

He really went downhill the last six months of
his life. He lost at least ten pounds, and I think
he got the dog equivalent of Alzheimer's.

He often seemed to be confused.

One night, he was in the front yard and wandered across the street.

I called him, but he wouldn't come.

After about five minutes, I went inside to get a flashlight.

He was in a neighbor's yard two houses over, and when I approached him, he spooked, obviously not recognizing me.

Finally, I knelt down, and he came to me!

When he was eleven, Kate (his momma) died (age 14), then a year later, so did Cheech (age 10).

Now he was alone in the backyard, and I think he was depressed.

This past duck season, our second period closed on Christmas Eve (my birthday).

I decided to take Jake on an easy afternoon hunt.

He was twelve and hadn't hunted for two years.

It was a warm, clear day.

We had a flooded millet field on some new land I had bought, and quite a few ducks had been using it.

I parked my SUV, unloaded the four-wheeler, then idled the quarter mile to the blind.

He ambled along, and I watched him closely to be sure I wasn't going too fast.

There was a time when he would jog three miles beside the four-wheeler!

I parked it on the levee, and we walked
the hundred yards to the blind.

He immediately jumped on his dog stand, I loaded
my gun and sat down on the bench.

Things were slow, but I enjoyed being out there with him.

Visions of the many great hunts we had
shared flooded my thoughts.

His eyes were scanning the skies, and I marveled
at his power of concentration!

He seemed to sense that this was his last hunt, and
he wasn't going to let anything slip up on us.

Over the years, there had been countless times when I followed his
stare to find ducks descending to the blocks on cupped wings!

With just two minutes of shooting time
left, I started unloading my gun.

Suddenly my peripheral vision picked up movement!

A drake pintail was making a wide circle around the decoys!

As he sailed by the outside edge of them, I
sensed that this was my only chance!

But when I stood to shoot, I realized that he was
way out there, probably out of range!

In desperation, I led him what seemed like an
incredible amount and squeezed the trigger!

At the shot, he set his wings and sailed across
the field, getting lower and lower!

He hit the ground just over a levee, at least
250 yards away, close to a big tree!

I don't think Jake ever saw him.

I told him, "Come on, Jake. Let's see if you can still find a duck!"

We walked to the four-wheeler, then motored slowly
around to where I had marked the duck's fall.

Jake was alert, but had no clue we were going on a search.

By this time, it was well after shooting time, so
my gun was unloaded and in its case.

A quick scan of the ground didn't show anything.

I got off the four-wheeler, knelt down, and said, "Find him, Jake!"

His look of amazement made me laugh!

If dogs could talk, he undoubtedly would have
said, "Who, me? I'm old! I'm retired!"

He looked to me for directions, and I sent him
into the edge of the woods along the levee.

As we had done innumerable times, I was
encouraging him with, "Find it! Find it, Jake!"

All of a sudden, he got "birdy," reversed his course, followed
his nose, and leaned down into a fallen treetop!

Sure enough, he rose up with a beautiful, very-much-alive pintail drake in his mouth!

Tears streamed down my face as this once proud warrior brought the duck to me, tail up and prancing!

I knew that this was his last duck!

Jake got to ride across my lap on the four-wheeler ride back to my SUV!

He had earned it!

In January, the vet said Jake needed surgery to remove some cysts.

He told us we would need to keep him in the garage for about two weeks.

The surgery went well, and I picked him up and drove him home.

He was as friendly as always, none too worse for the wear.

I laid out a blanket for him in the garage, and he seemed content to be right there.

My wife and I closed the garage door and went out for dinner in my SUV.

At that time, our son-in-law was living with us, and foolishly I hadn't told him about our garage guest.

When he came home, he opened the garage door and went inside, leaving the garage door open, not knowing that Jake was in there (Jake didn't greet him).

Evidently he decided to take a stroll, since
he was gone when we got back.

My guess is that he got disoriented and couldn't
figure out how to get back home.

Cantrell Road is a very busy street, and he was
simply in the wrong place at the wrong time.

I buried him on a rise overlooking Pipkin
Lake, beside Suzie, Kate, and Cheech.

In my mind, this fall, they will all be watching
us hunt out of the middle blind, wishing they were with us!

Good job, big man. I love you!

Whiskey on an Island

By Rudy Martin

Several men decided that they wanted to go on a float trip on the Little Red River. They were Henry Gregory, Taylor McAdams, Ira Foster, and my dad. They got my best friend, Alwyn Dalrymple, to agree to paddle the supply boat.

Mr. McAdams and Mr. Foster put in first, followed by Mr. Gregory and Dad. The first day, they caught a lot of smallmouths, and they made camp on a sandbar. The meal was great, and plenty of whiskey was flowing.

Mr. Gregory decided to pitch his cot on a ledge about twenty yards from the gravel bar (some said he had been drinking!).

Everybody slept well, and they were ready to shove off just after daylight. They picked out another gravel bar early, about noon.

Needless to say, it wouldn't be getting dark for several hours, so the libations started flowing early!

By three o'clock, everybody was as drunk as a skunk, and Dad announced that they only had one pint of whiskey left!

None of the men trusted each other to safeguard that whiskey, so they took Alwyn out in the river and left him on a small island with the whiskey!

Then they chained the boat up, and my dad was entrusted with the key!

So there they were on a float trip that wouldn't end for two more days! Dad knew every bootlegger around there, so he volunteered to walk down a gravel road to buy some whiskey.

He returned three hours later with half a case of whiskey!

The other guys descended on it like a pack of wolves!

Somebody unchained the boat and rescued Alwyn off the island, and he ate a dozen fried eggs!

The rest of the float was uneventful, but they all said that they wanted to do it every year from now on!

Where Oh Where

By Rudy Martin

I grew up an Episcopalian. There the young
boys that served were called acolytes.

In the Catholic church, the young boys
that serve are called altar boys.

The training for the altar boys was much harder for the
boys to catch on to than what the acolytes had to learn,
and the priests got very upset if an altar boy messed up!

It was this altar boy's first Sunday to serve, and he was very nervous!

Things went well until the time came for the altar boy
to bring the priest the Incense Pot, and he froze!

The priest saw that the altar boy was terrified, so
he put his request in the form of a chant!

He chanted, "Where oh where is the Incense Pot?"

No response!

He chanted again, "Where oh where is the Incense Pot?"

No response!

He chanted the third time, "Where oh where is the Incense Pot?"

No response!

Then the altar boy chanted, "I left it outside 'cause it's too damn hot!"

Where Did the Snakes Go?

By Rudy Martin

My dad and I were fishing Indian bayou. It's near Saint Charles, Arkansas. It's a running bayou, and we loved catching Kentucky bass there in the current. It had a lot of steep red clay banks, and the Kentucky bass loved to get right up against those banks and feed on crawfish.

To get there, we kept a johnboat at Homer Stark's dock at Crockett's Bluff near Stuttgart, and it had a Martin 7 1/2HP motor on it. The motor had a neutral gear, and that was useful because we always fished going upstream. When the man in the front of the boat got a strike, the one in the back would put the motor in neutral so the boat wouldn't go over unfished waters.

We were fishing a red clay bank early one Saturday morning when two large cottonmouth moccasins slid into the water off the bank and went under swimming directly toward our boat!

I was in the front, and Dad was in the back, and both of us were scanning the water to see where those snakes were going to come up!

He put the running motor in neutral.

All of a sudden, the boat rocked violently from side to side. I turned around, and Dad was as white as a sheet!

He said that when the snakes appeared, he let go of the tiller to see what they were going to do. All of a sudden, something poked him in the side and wiggled, and he thought that was one of those snakes getting ready to bite him! It was the vibrating tiller that poked him in the side!

Dad put the motor in gear, and we sped away!

Wastebasket

By Rudy Martin

My wife was a redhead, and she fit the perception that all redheads are feisty and will pounce on you in a nanosecond!

We had only been married for two weeks when she interrupted my TV watching and proceeded to chew me out over some piddling thing!

She said she hated me and would be getting a divorce!

I got up and retreated to our bedroom, but she followed me and continued yapping at me!

I got a suitcase out of the closet and started packing, thinking that this is the worst day of my life!

That didn't slow down the yapping one bit—she yelled even louder!

She left the room, then came back in about thirty minutes later.

She said she wanted to sit in my lap, and I let her.

She wanted to kiss and fondle me, saying she was so sorry she acted the way that she did and she didn't want us to break up.

We were married twenty-three years.

I'm a big duck hunter, and duck season is on during the Christmas holidays.

It was Saturday, and Dad and I went hunting that morning.

We were invited to a very nice dinner at
the Pine Bluff Country Club.

I wanted to get a good nap in so I would be lively for the party.

I was just dozing off when the door flew open
and she charged into the bedroom!

She proceeded to tell me that she was sick and
tired of putting up with the evils of duck season,
and she demanded that I never go again!

That red hair was blazing, and she was shaking her finger at me!

She made one final point, whirled around,
and stepped right in the wastebasket!

Needless to say, I lost it, and that made her even madder!

The vision I had when she stumbled through the door trying
to shake off that wastebasket will always be in my memory!

Uncle Lara

By Rudy Martin

My dad grew up in a big three-story house in Pine Bluff, Arkansas.

His mother (Suzie Martin) took in boarders and also served a delicious noon meal. All of the family called her Nannie.

Dad's best friend was Mr. Lara Hutt. They were best man in each other's wedding.

Both of them worked for Simmons Bank then (they were in side-by-side booths).

And both of them loved to fish and duck hunt, and they let me tag along!

The boarding house had a circular driveway through a brick entrance, and Nannie had always wanted a gate there.

Dad decided to surprise her and give her a gate for Christmas. He had a bricklayer do it, and it looked great!

Dad and Nannie were eating breakfast on Christmas day when they heard this horrible crash!

Dad ran outside, and Uncle Lara was beside himself because he wasn't looking for a gate, and he demolished it! To make matters worse, he was coming over to show Dad his new car!

Too Much Sex

By Rudy Martin

A young couple went to a ski lodge for their honeymoon.

They stayed in their room for three days, and the husband said he was going to go skiing.

The young bride said, "Honey, I'm embarrassed that you're going to see a bunch of people, but they won't be seeing me.

They'll know what we've been doing!"

The husband said, "I tell you what, I'll put on my ski togs, climb out of the window, and ski around to the main area. The people will see me, and they'll think you're right around the corner."

She said, "Okay."

He did just that, and when he got to the main area, he turned sideways and threw up a lot of snow when he stopped.

Everybody was kind of startled that he did that, so their attention was on him.

He smiled and said, "Hi, everybody. You know, anybody who doesn't like to screw is a skiball!"

Too Many Children

By Rudy Martin

Back in the days when passengers boarded a flight, they walked out on the tarmac and stepped up a ladder to board.

I was about halfway to the plane when the children that were holding the hands of a woman in front of me bolted!

She took off after the boy, so I took off after the girl!

When I got to her, I scooped her into my arms and said, "Hi, I'm Rudy."

She said, "Hi, Mr. Rudy."

I followed her mother up the stairs and to their seats.

She said, "Thank you so much. I don't know what I'd have done without you."

I said, "I enjoyed doing it. I love kids."

After we took off, the little girl stood up in her seat and smiled at me.

I smiled back, and she said to her mother, "Mommy, can I sit with that man?"

I got out of my seat, got the approval nod from the mother, and took the girl to my seat.

She had brought some crayons, so we colored some things in the flight book.

Then she said, "I'm sleepy," and she spent the rest of the flight asleep in my arms.

Tears were running down my cheeks when I gave her back to her mother.

Thank you, God, for that opportunity.

Tabasco

By Rudy Martin

My friend Alf Williams loves to play practical jokes on me.

We belong to a duck hunting club near Sherrill, Arkansas.

Teal season is always in September, and we decided to come to our clubhouse for the weekend and hunt them.

The last time anybody had been in our clubhouse was in February when duck season ended.

We had cleaned out all the perishables in February, but we missed one item!

We sat down for supper on Friday night, and I had gotten us some fried catfish.

Alf always puts lots of Tabasco sauce on fish, but the regular red sauce bottle was missing, and there was only an obviously old bottle of it. It had turned green and had lumps in it!

Alf proceeded to put lots of that green slime on his fish, and he was laughing at me.

I ran to the bathroom and threw up!

On my way to the head, Alf yelled, "This is delicious. I put some on your fish!"

Three Dogs

By Rudy Martin

Three dogs were running down an alley. They were in a thunderstorm, running through sheets of water.

One of the dogs was about six feet in front of the other two, and every step it took threw mud and water all over the two in the back.

One of the dogs in the back said to the other one, "Man, ain't this a bitch," and the other one said, "It better be!"

There's a Fish in His Arm

By Rudy Martin

When my daughter Paula was twelve, she and all her friends were playing on the swing set in our yard when everybody but Paula came running in, yelling, "Paula's hurt, Paula's hurt, Paula's hurt!"

I ran outside, and Paula was crying. I could tell by the way her arm was twisted that it was broken.

I brought her inside, fashioned a sling for her arm, put her in my car, and took her to the emergency room of Davis Hospital.

It was about thirty minutes before the doctor took her into an examining room, and Paula had stopped crying.

A black man came walking down the hall and went into one of the examining rooms.

Paula said, "Dad, that man had a fish in his arm!"

I thought, *Oh brother, Paula has lost it. She's in shock!*

So I said, "Honey, I didn't see a fish. Just relax and we'll see the doctor in a few minutes."

After a few minutes, the black man walked by us and went out the front door of the clinic.

One of the nurses approached us and said, "Y'all aren't going to believe this, but that man was fishing, got a bite, jerked a catfish out of the water, and one of its spiny fins got wedged between the wristbones of the man's hand. The doctor had to clip it off!"

So Paula wasn't in shock at all. She was telling the truth!

The Pendleton Invitational

By Rudy Martin

I went to work for IBM in Memphis, Tennessee, after I graduated from the University of Arkansas in Fayetteville, Arkansas.

I was flattered that IBM chose me over several other candidates.

My dad started taking me duck hunting when I was five years old, starting with a BB Gun.

My dad and his best friend, Lara Hutt (Uncle Lara), built a modest clubhouse by buying three ten-by-twenty officer's cabins they found at Camp Robinson.

They knocked out the front of one of them and the back of another one and attached them together.

Then they built a long screened porch and attached the ten-by-twenty and the ten-by-ten cabins to it.

We slept in the ten-by-twenty cabin, and the ten-by-ten one was where we cooked.

I spent many nights in that cabin duck hunting and fishing.

We thought it was a palace!

It was located on little Lennox Lake, near Dumas, Arkansas.

We killed lots of ducks and caught lots of bass there.

As I said, I was living in Memphis, and it's about
150 miles from Memphis to the clubhouse.

Of course, that's way too far to get up in the morning
in Memphis and get to the lake before shooting
time, so we came down the night before.

One spring, I had the bright idea to have what
I called the Pendleton Invitational.

I named it that because there was a ferry on the Arkansas
River that ferried vehicles across the river.

It was held on the Fourth of July.

Several of us set up a ping-pong table,
horseshoes, badminton, and volleyball.

I bought small trophies for a men's winner, a men's runner-up,
a women's winner, and a women's runner-up for every sport.

We cooked hamburgers and hot dogs on a grill.

Unfortunately, it was blazing hot on the fourth, over a hundred!

If it hadn't been for the cold beer consumed,
it would have been dangerous!

The women quit playing, but the men kept right on going.

We held it every year for several years.

The Bumalo House

By Rudy Martin

The plan was for the three of us to meet at Gordon's house before daylight on Saturday, then take one vehicle to fish the McGeorge stick pond.

It was 1968, and my friends—Gordon Bridges, a farmer who lived in the country in a wide place in the road named Cornerstone, Arkansas, and Alwyn Dalrymple, an insurance agent who lived in Little Rock—invited me to go fishing with them. I lived in Pine Bluff.

The McGeorge family of Pine Bluff has extensive farming interests around Cornerstone, and their stick pond is a dead-timber reservoir of about four hundred acres.

I had heard about it all my life, but had never seen it.

Supposedly the fishing for largemouth bass was outstanding.

Needless to say, I was pumped at the prospect of fishing a primo place.

I arrived at Gordon's house about ten minutes ahead of the agreed-upon hour.

Alwyn's car was there, but Gordon's truck was nowhere to be seen.

The lights were on in the kitchen, and the back door was unlocked.

When I walked into the house, the warm, pungent smell of coffee filled my nostrils.

Thinking the two of them had gone to pick something
up and would be right back, I settled into a chair.

But after waiting fifteen minutes, I realized those SOBS had
gone on without me (they must have forgotten I was coming)!

So there I was, out in the country, in the pitch-black dark,
with no idea how to get to the McGeorge stick pond!

Predictably, my bulldog personality convinced me that the thing to
do was to try to find someone who was awake and get directions.

I wasn't about to give up and drive home.

Gordon's wife, Pat, was undoubtedly in the house,
but I didn't feel right waking her up.

Besides, she might not know where the stick pond was.

So I got in my car and started looking for
a house with their lights on.

Before long, I spotted a small, very old ramshackle
house that had lights on inside.

I had some reservations about going up to the front door,
but I persuaded myself that if I left my headlights on and the
engine running, whoever was inside wouldn't feel threatened.

Hoping for the best, I parked in the front and
shuffled onto the rickety wooden porch.

After a knock or two on the front door, a man's
voice from inside said, "What do you want?"

Then the following dialogue went on, all through the closed front door:

"I'm trying to find the McGeorge stick pond."

"You can't miss it."

"Well, I've missed it so far. Can you tell me where to go?"

"You turn left down there by the bumalo house."

"The what?"

"The bumalo house, down there by the sign."

Thinking there was a sign that said McGeorge stick pond, I asked, "What does the sign say?"

"It used to say stop, but it don't say nothin' now."

"Okay, once I turn left. How far is it?"

"Not too far."

"How far did you say it was?"

"It ain't very far."

Exasperated, I thanked him and struck out for parts unknown.

So there I was, looking for some sort of house at an intersection that had an unreadable sign, at which I was to turn left and travel an unknown distance.

Simple.

But sure enough, shortly I came to an intersection, and my headlights illuminated a large one-story wooden house with a screened-in front porch that I later found out was known locally as the bungalow house.

And on the corner was a weathered red metal sign that undoubtedly used to stay

Stop.

I optimistically turned left, not knowing if I was going to travel half a mile or ten.

The road was gravel, and I went about three miles before coming to a locked cable stretched across the road, blocking my vehicle.

It was just beginning to get daylight, and I could see what looked like a levee a couple of hundred yards past the cable.

Gathering up my fishing tackle, I stepped over the cable and walked toward the levee.

Almost immediately, I came to an old red caboose off to the side of the road.

Having grown up as an avid duck hunter, I had heard stories of McGeorge hunting parties using the caboose as a place to gather before their hunt.

Thus, I was confident that I was at least on McGeorge property.

Once I climbed the levee, what was undoubtedly the McGeorge stick pond lay in front of me.

There were several trucks parked there, including Gordon's.

Of course, Gordon and Alwyn were long gone, busily fishing away.

It was after daylight now, but I couldn't
see any boats on the reservoir.

Without much hope, I hollered Gordon's
name a few times, to no avail.

Then I realized that the reservoir had a large
mowed levee all the way around it.

If only the keys were in Gordon's truck,
maybe I could find the guys!

Sure enough, they were in the ignition, and after loading my
fishing stuff in the back of his truck, I struck out after them.

Of course, I could go right or left, so on a whim, I went right.

I hadn't gone but a few hundred yards when I
spied them fishing in Gordon's boat.

Success at last!

As I pulled up beside them (me on the levee, them down
in the reservoir), I clearly heard Gordon say to Alwyn,

"Hey, some SOB is driving my truck."

I leaned out the window and yelled, "Yeah, me!" They both
did a double take, and Alwyn said, "Oh no, we left him!"

They quickly pulled over to the bank,
and I joined them in the boat.

They were practically hysterical with laughter
when I told them all that had happened!

Both had completely forgotten that I was to meet them.

We had a great fishing trip, catching a bunch of nice bass.

And we told a few stories along the way.

So there you have it, my quest to find the
infamous McGeorge stick pond.

And it would never have happened without the bumalo house.

Tees

By Rudy Martin

A man bought a new Chrysler and stopped at
a filling station to fill it up with gas.

The man looked at the brand-new car and said, "Wow, Mr.
Cook. That sure is a fine-looking automobile you have!"

The owner said, "Yes, it's got about everything you can put on it."

The owner was a golfer, and he had some golf tees on the seat.

The filling station man said, "What are those things on the seat?"

The owner said, "Those are tees. You put your
balls on them when you are driving."

The service station man said, "Uh-um, them
Chrysler folks think of everything!"

Suzie's Longest Retrieve

By Rudy Martin

My dad and I went duck hunting one Saturday morning on Pipkin Lake near Sherrill, Arkansas. We killed six ringnecks. Ringnecks are a fast-flying diving duck, and they love to fly about six feet above the water.

Many times, I've shot at the lead duck and killed the third one back.

I had Suzie with me. Her grandfather was a lab named Super Chief, who won two national field trials.

When we finished our hunt, I got in my car and was driving to Gillette, Arkansas, to be with Bill Tedford, who had invited me to hunt with him Saturday afternoon and Sunday morning. It was really cold the night before, and all the flooded fields were frozen.

I was between Stuttgart and Dewitt when I saw a dead snow goose lying in a flooded field on top of the ice about 150 yards from the highway. I had worked really hard teaching my lab whistle and hand signals, so I decided to see if I could get her to bring me that goose.

I parked on the shoulder of the highway and got Suzie out of her kennel. I gave her a heel command, and she immediately got on my left side, with her muzzle about even with my knee.

Of course, she didn't know anything about the goose, but I wanted to give it a shot. I lined her muzzle up with the goose and said, "Back!"

I'd taught her to run in a straight line, so she took off in a dead run.

She got about 100 yards from me and veered a little to the left of the goose, so I blew a sharp blast on my whistle, and she instantly whirled around and sat down facing me.

I took a step to my right, stuck out my right arm, and gave her an "Over!" command. She immediately took off to my right. When she got in line with the goose, I stopped her with my whistle. The goose was still at least 80 yards away. I put my left hand in my pocket and my right arm up over my head and gave her a "Back!" command. She whirled around and took off at a dead run in the direction of the goose.

She veered a little off course, and I was getting ready to correct her when she tucked her tail, ran straight to the goose, and brought it to me!

Evidently, a puff of wind blew for a few seconds from the goose to her, and it was game over!

Super Chief would have been proud of his granddaughter!

Stranded

By Rudy Martin

There was skim ice around the bank of
the lake as we got into the boat.

The thermometer at the trailer showed twenty-eight degrees.

This was shaping up as a banner day for us, since the rice fields around us would likely be frozen, while the lake would be open.

I suggested that we hunt a blind on the lake
that hadn't been hunted as yet.

It's only about 300 yards from our trailer, but it's tucked against the buckbrush in an area mallards like.

It turned out that we were the only ones who hunted that Sunday morning, but at that time, that was fine with us.

It was the Thanksgiving Week of 1998, and my fiancée, Mary Jane, and I stayed at our trailer on Pipkin Lake on my farm near Sherrill, Arkansas.

We were both in our late fifties, with grown children,
yet we eagerly looked forward to a life together.

The trailer was a 28' pull-type, with a generator,
central heating system, and indoor plumbing.

The duck season had opened the previous Saturday, so we decided to stay there from Wednesday night through Sunday afternoon.

The Friday after Thanksgiving was always slow at the
office, so I looked forward to a long, relaxing time.

The duck hunting was excellent on Thursday, Friday,
and Saturday. Several other members of the club
had already hunted, with limits the norm.

We had hunted the main blind twice, and I wanted other
members to get a chance to hunt it on Sunday morning.

The blind we hunted is a large floater, designed so
the boat goes behind it under a boat hide.

The lake was high from an influx of water from the Arkansas
River, and the 8' decoy strings were barely touching the bottom.

I've always used a brick on a rope to keep the boat under the boat
hide, and as we pulled in, I noticed that the brick was gone.

I let the fact that ducks were already flying distract me, and
we got into the blind without my securing the boat.

As we were getting our guns out of their cases,
I looked out, and there was the boat, about ten
yards from the blind and floating away!

But it was just after daylight, and I was convinced
that someone else would be coming to hunt.

They could retrieve our boat for us.

Jumping into deep water and having to swim was not what I
wanted to do, so I made the decision to wait for another hunter!

We watched as our boat drifted clear across the
lake, with me not being too concerned.

Unfortunately for us, my cell phone was on the seat of
my Isuzu trooper, which was parked at the trailer.

We killed five mallards and two green-winged teal,
with my chocolate lab, Jake, doing the honors.

Two of them fell dead well away from the blind,
and I marked them for future pickup.

By eight, it was apparent that no one else was coming to hunt!

We shared a thermos of coffee and devoured
two packages of peanut butter crackers.

By noon, it was clear to me that we would have no
choice except to spend the night in the blind!

I knew it would be a cold, miserable night,
but what else could we do?

It was about twenty yards to a heavy stand of
buckbrush (which was about ten yards wide) and
then another thirty yards to shallow water.

From there, it was another hundred yards
through shallow water to the dry ground!

Hunting on the lake is generally not good in the afternoon,
so the chance of a member coming down that afternoon was
slim to none. Maybe a deer hunter would come down, but if
so, there wasn't any reason for them to come to the lake.

Now I started kicking myself, a seasoned
hunter, for making a rookie mistake!

I'm a good swimmer, but I knew that the buckbrush would be tough to get through—not strong enough to support me but dense enough to be a problem!

And at age 59, I wasn't sure what effect jumping in the cold water would have on me!

It was rare for members to hunt on Mondays, so we had to count on my son Al missing us and coming down to investigate.

There was no doubt in my mind he would do this eventually, but we had no way of knowing how long that would be!

I had some matches and a candle in my shell box, but everything in the blind was made of wood except the roof, which was corrugated roofing.

Starting a fire would be no problem; keeping the blind from catching on fire would be!

We talked about various things as the hours dragged slowly by, rationing the last of the coffee.

Mostly we discussed our rescue: How long it would take Al to figure out something was wrong, and would a member of the deer camp on the far side of the lake show up to hunt?

As predicted, no ducks flew in the afternoon, and we watched a beautiful sunset followed by total darkness.

My flashlight was right beside my cell phone in the trooper!

It was cold, with a blustery wind from the west.

Jake was restless, but he stayed right there with us.

I gave him permission, and he promptly relieved himself both ways on the floor of the blind.

I exchanged jackets with Mary Jane when she complained of the being cold, so I built a safe fire!

Clearing off a place on the metal roof, I gathered some brush and started it.

It was only about the size of a salad plate, but it provided visual and emotional comfort.

We stayed busy talking and stoking the flames with brush off the blind.

Suddenly one of the roof supports started smoking! I used the top to the thermos to splash lake water on it until it went out! It was a tense moment, and I had a mental image of the blind catching on fire, with us being forced to swim for it in total darkness!

The view of the stars and moon was gorgeous, although we didn't properly appreciate it under the circumstances.

We could hear traffic on a paved road about half a mile away, but the Arkansas River levee was between the road and us.

Mary Jane suggested that we yell and/or fire our guns, but I felt it was pointless since we were completely shielded from their view.

About ten, we decided to try to get some sleep.

I made sure the fire was out, then each of us stretched out on a bench.

That didn't work, so we ended up huddling on a bench under the roof in the west corner of the blind, where the plywood side protected us from the west wind.

Mary Jane was closest to the wall. I had my arm around her, and she put Jake across her lap! Fortunately we had dressed appropriately for the cold weather, so it was bearable!

I'm very hot natured, so I was okay, but Mary Jane shivered throughout the night!

She said later that Jake was a godsend, as his body heat transferred warmth to her.

I woke up many times during the night and was amazed to realize that the position of the moon and stars had changed!

Of course it's obvious that it was due to the earth's rotation, but I had never thought about that.

Just before daylight, Mary Jane started really shivering!

I had read that uncontrollable shivering was one of the first signs of hypothermia.

I removed my chamois shirt and insisted that she put it on under her jacket.

She didn't want to unzip her jacket and get colder, but I persisted until she did!

Knowing that the coldest time of the day is just before daylight, I was confident she would be better off when daylight came. Eventually her shivering subsided.

When daylight did come, the decoys were covered with frost, and I could see some skim ice around the buckbrush!

Fortunately, I was comfortable with just a long underwear top and her jacket.

Mary Jane had no interest in trying to shoot a duck.

She jokingly chastised me for hunting in those conditions, but ducks were flying and Jake and I were alert and ready!

I shot two wood ducks and one mallard.

True to my guess, no members came to hunt.

We were faced with the two options we had the previous day—swim for it or wait for my son Al!

My gut feeling was that he would come for us by Tuesday night, but I wasn't sure Mary Jane could get through another night! The weather forecast was for clear and cold for several days, so we would have to face another night like the one we had just experienced!

I didn't have enough experience with hypothermia to know how much trouble she had been in, so I was very reluctant to subject her to that again!

Around ten thirty, it was about as warm as I thought it would get for the day, so I decided to swim out!

I took off my jacket and gloves, but left my insulated hunting pants on (my first mistake)! The short L. L. Bean boots I had on had felt inserts in them, and I took them out and put the boots back on (my second mistake)! My logic was that once I got to where I could stand, I would have to walk 300 yards to the trailer, and I didn't want to do that in my boots with no socks.

Just before I got in the water, I debated on what to say to Mary Jane!

I wanted to tell her that if something happened to me, she was to stay put until Al came!

She would have another jacket, another pair of gloves, and the felt inserts, so she would be able to survive!

I chose not to say anything. She told me later that she wouldn't have been able to handle any discussion about something happening to me.

My plan was to sit on the floor of the blind and slowly submerge my body to get it accustomed to the cold water, but that didn't work!

Realizing it was now or never, I jumped into the icy water in the boat hide stall! The water was a shock to my system, but to my relief, I was able to function!

The first twenty yards to the buckbrush came pretty easily, with me using a breaststroke and scissors kick. I grabbed hold of a willow limb to hang on to where the buckbrush started and paused to catch my breath.

Mary Jane was standing on a bench trying to see me, but her view was blocked!

"I'm okay," I yelled, "just resting for a minute!"

"Be careful!" she yelled back.

When I started through the buckbrush, it was just like I thought—thick and hard to swim or pull through!

Finally I got through it and paused again, gasping for air!

I realized then that I wasn't really too uncomfortable in the cold water, and that I should slow down and not exert so much energy!

I had been in the water for no more than three minutes, and I had read that you were all right for about twenty minutes!

"I'm okay," I yelled again to Mary Jane. "Resting up for the final push!"

"Where are you?" she inquired.

"Through the buckbrush, and I can see the shallow water," I replied.

By this time, the insulated pants were waterlogged and extremely heavy, and of course, the boots were also full! I could see a sprig of milo about twenty-five yards in front of me!

I knew that milo never grows more than about three feet high!

I couldn't touch the bottom where I was, but somewhere between that milo and me, it would be shallow enough for me to stand!

Summoning all my remaining energy, I struck out for the milo!

But my lower half was so heavy, I was sinking completely underwater between breaststrokes!

I knew I was in immediate peril!

I switched to a crawl stroke with a flutter kick, but I felt my muscles tiring rapidly!

"Come on, you sissy, you can make it!" I cried out in desperation!

When I thought I couldn't take another stroke, I decided to stop kicking and see if I could make progress by going under and pushing off the bottom!

After doing this a few times, suddenly my chin was barely out of the water with my feet on the bottom!

I yelled to Mary Jane, "My feet are on the bottom," and she yelled back, "Praise the Lord!"

Now that I was standing, I needed to get to the dry ground!

The shortest route to dry ground was about 100 yards, and it lay right in front of me, but there was an ominous space about ten yards wide with no milo! Sensing that this was a deep spot through which I probably couldn't swim, I opted for a diagonal path of about 250 yards toward the trailer where I could see milo the whole way. When I reached the dry ground, Mary Jane's dog, Charley, greeted me! We had left her outside the trailer, and she had spent the night on her own!

I trudged the remaining yards to the trailer and immediately started the generator, which kicked on the fan for the propane central heating unit! Knowing that Mary Jane would hear the generator and know I was okay, I went inside, toweled off, and put on dry clothes!

Strangely, after I finished getting dressed, I started shaking, so I wrapped a goose down sleeping bag around my shoulders and sat on the edge of the bed for a few minutes.

I guess my adrenaline had quit pumping, and the reality of what was a close call I had gone through was sinking in! But I couldn't afford the luxury of what-if right now—I had a cold, tired fiancée to rescue!

After a few minutes, I was fine, so I walked down
the hill and bailed out the other boat.

The motor started on the second pull, and
I set out to pick up Mary Jane!

We loaded our gear and Jake into the boat and
headed for the trailer! She pointed out that the
water bowl for the dogs still had ice in it!

Then she said, "Let's eat!" While she fixed us a
sumptuous breakfast, I retrieved the three ducks
killed the day before and the runaway boat!

When we got home, we found that my
son had indeed been trailing us!

He had called my office Monday morning, and
they said they hadn't heard from me!
Then he got the same message at lunchtime, plus there
was no answer at the house or my cell phone!

He had made up his mind to come looking
for us if we weren't home by dark!

We ended up spending twenty-eight hours stranded in that blind!

In retrospect, would it have been better for me to have jumped
in the water immediately, pulled the boat to the blind, then
gone to the trailer to warm up and get dry clothes?

Was getting in the water at any time during
this ordeal the right thing to do?

What if I had been unable to breathe in the water or
had a heart attack? What if I had drowned?

What if Mary Jane had been unable to withstand another night in the blind?

What if my son had been out of town?

Lots of questions, few answers!

Nature can be harsh and unforgiving, so watch your p's and q's and don't tempt fate!

Never Own a Two-Door Car

By Rudy Martin

Two men were running their trap lines when they found a bobcat that was caught in a trap.

He was not a happy camper!

One of the men was getting ready to kill the bobcat when the other man yelled, "Wait, wait, wait! Instead of killing him, let's go get our toolbox, put him in it, and take him to the zoo!"

The other man agreed, and they went to their truck, took out all the tools in it, and took it to where the bobcat was. They turned their toolbox upside down and managed to get the bobcat in it.

They got back to their trapline, got the rest of their stuff, and headed for their truck.

Just as they got to their truck, a black two-door car pulled up behind their toolbox and put it in their car and took off!

The trappers jumped in their truck and started honking like hell trying to get the car to stop!

This went on for about a quarter of a mile when the car suddenly left the road, went through a barbed wire fence, and stopped.

The bobcat jumped out and ran away!

The driver jumped out and ran away, but
the other one couldn't get out!

The trappers started cussing the other man, and
he said he couldn't get out of the car!

He looked like he had tried to run through a barbed wire fence!

He was scratched and bleeding in dozens of places!

He said, "Gentlemen, all I can say is, I'll
always hate a two-door car!"

Nancy Hunt

By Rudy Martin

I played tennis for the U of A—lettered three years.

In those days, the U of A didn't have enough money to play the other teams in the Southwest Conference, so we played teams from local colleges—Southwest Missouri State, Drury College, Springfield Tech, etc.

Although we didn't play them in the round-robin, the rules permitted the U of A to have two players in the Southwest Conference champion tennis tournament, which was played at the Fort Worth Country Club.

My senior year, they sent Jay Dickey (a junior) and me.

Both of us lost in the first round, but we got to the semifinals in doubles.

The team we were playing consisted of Ronnie Fisher, who had beaten Barry McKay, the number 1 player in the country, and David Young, the number 3 junior (he was eighteen) in the country behind Butch Buchholtz and Chuck McKinley!

There was a big gallery watching, and they beat us 19–17, 7–5!

Both of us played way over our heads! Any other day they would have beaten us 6–0, 6–0!

The score was tied 14–14, and Ronnie hit a blistering serve wide to my backhand!

I hit it late, and it went down the alley for a clean winner!

Jay said, "Did you mean to do that?" I
said, "Hell no! But I'll take it!"

After the match, we went to our motel, and Jay called a chi-o he knew named Mary Shoptaw. It was Friday, and he asked her for a date. She accepted and told Jay she would get me a date.

She said they would pick us up at the hotel at seven.

At seven, a new Mercedes convertible drove up, and a tall, good-looking blonde got out of the convertible and said, "Hi, I'm Nancy Hunt, and you must be Rudy."

I said, "Yes," and she put me in the front seat of the car with her and Jay and his date in the back seat.

She said she would drive, and that was fine with me.

She said, "Let's go to Cattleman's, a famous restaurant."

Neither Jay nor I had much money on us, and we were unsure if we had enough money to pay the check!

The valet parking man said, "Hello, Ms. Hunt," and so did the maître d'.

My wheels started turning. *How do these people know her?*

It turned out that she was the grandniece of the richest man in America—H. L. Hunt!

Everybody ordered T-bone steaks. They were delicious!

When the check came, Nancy produced a diner's club card and paid for everything!

She asked me to drive, and I said, "Nancy, I don't know how to get to our hotel."
She said, "Don't be silly. I want y'all to drop us off at the chi-o house and keep my car for the weekend! We'll come out and watch all of your matches!"

They did, and she gave me a big kiss when we got in the taxi to go to the airport!

From then on, we met to watch the football game between SMU and the U of A. If it was in Dallas, I traveled to her. If it was in Fayetteville, she traveled to me.

We fell deeply in love!

When we both graduated, we exchanged Christmas cards and letters for a while, then we gradually drifted apart—she moved to New York, and I moved to Memphis.

I attended an IBM sales class in Endicott, New York.

Two of us that attended were single, and we decided to spend a week in New York and Atlantic City.

I decided to try to contact Nancy. I didn't have her phone number, but I remembered her parents' address in Houston.

They wouldn't do this now, but I talked the operator into looking at all the addresses of Hunts in Houston, and she found it!

So I called person-to-person for Nancy Hunt, and the person who answered the phone said, "She doesn't live here anymore. She lives in New York!

Duh!

That person gave me her phone number
in New York, and I called it!

She answered, and after some oohing and aahing, she asked me
where we were staying, and I told her we hadn't decided yet!

She put her hand over the phone, and I
heard her talking to someone.

She said that she and her boyfriend were going out of town
for a few days, and we could stay in his apartment!

We did, and we had an absolute blast!

We never talked again!

Mr. Howard Bartlett

By Rudy Martin

Mr. Howard Bartlett was a farmer friend of my dad.

He made a lot of money selling produce to local grocery stores.

He liked to come into the bank and drink coffee and listen to my dad telling him jokes.

Mr. Howard could be funny without trying to be. He just talked about what he saw!

Dad said that one day they were in the coffee shop when a very, very skinny woman walked by and Mr. Howard said, "Wow, getting in bed with her would be like getting in bed with a bunch of welding tools!"

He hunted with us a lot on Pipkin Lake, and when things got slow, he'd get me to take him to the bank of the lake so he could look around.

Out of curiosity, I stayed with him one day to see what he was seeing that was so interesting.

He'd walk slowly down the bank, taking in everything in sight.

When he got comfortable with me, he would tell me what he was seeing:

"Here's where a coon came by last night looking for something to eat.

A mink did the same thing as the coon around an hour later.

A covey of quail roosted here last night. All the quail face out so they can fly off if danger arrives."

It was fascinating!

My good friend Tabby Benton and one of Mr. Howard's daughters were in love. He had asked her to marry him, and she had accepted; but Tabby hadn't asked for Mr. Howard's permission!

Ann had told her mother, so she invited Tabby to have dinner with her family.

Mr. Howard loved his family, but he was the king of the hill when it came to who ruled the roost!

Nobody came to the table until Mr. Howard was seated.

He served all the plates, and you dared not take a bite until after he did!

Tabby told me that they were still seated when he got up his courage to ask Mr. Howard for Ann's hand.

Mr. Howard didn't say a word. He just said, "Come on, bigfoot" (that's what he called Tabby) and walked out the door.

Tabby said they drove down a gravel road a couple of miles without anyone saying anything.

Mr. Howard said, "Bigfoot, get us some kindling and put it in the middle of the road."

Tabby told me he did that, then Mr. Howard put some bigger limbs on it, poured some kerosene on it, and dropped a match on it.

Mr. Howard told big foot to sit down, and it was deathly quiet.

After about thirty minutes, Mr. Howard said, "I give you permission to marry Ann, but I don't want no drinkin' or runnin' around on her. Can you do that?"

Tabby told me that he said that he could do that, and with that, Mr. Howard kicked out the fire and drove them back to his house.

Monk

By Rudy Martin

This man decided that he wanted to become a monk. The discipline this monastery had was you couldn't say a word for ten years!

So the head monk called him in after ten years and said, "Okay, you can say two words!"

The monk said, "Food bad!" And the head monk said, "Nope, you're not ready. Go out and study ten more years!"

So the head monk called him in after twenty years and said, "Okay, you can say two words!"

The monk said, "Bed hard!" And the head monk said, "Nope, you're not ready. Go out and study ten more years!"

So the head monk called him in after thirty years and said, "Okay, you can say two words!"

The monk said, "I quit!" And the head monk said, "You might as well. You haven't done anything but bitch the whole time you've been here!"

Mongoose

By Rudy Martin

My friend Tommy Stobaugh loved to play practical jokes on people.

He got an orange crate, put hardware cloth over
part of it and plywood over the other part.

Another piece of plywood separated the crate
vertically, and he cut a semicircle halfway across the
plywood (like the mouse had in *Tom and Jerry*).

He put a squirrel's tail through the hole so that it
looked like some critter was in there. He had a string
attached to the tail, and it was attached to a spring!

Tommy had a spiel about how vicious a mongoose is! He tapped
on the crate a few times, but the mongoose wouldn't come out!

A man named Richard Bennett played football
for the Razorbacks. He was huge!

He got Richard to lean way over the crate,
and Tommy released the spring!

All hell broke loose!

Richard's knee hit me right in the chest, bowled me over, and
knocked the wind out of me—I couldn't catch my breath!

There were several fraternity brothers in the room, and they were dying laughing!

Richard had retreated to the bathroom!

He said that he hadn't been so scared in his life!

Miss America

By Rudy Martin

I went to work for IBM right out of college in 1960.

At lunchtime on my first day, three of the salesmen invited me to lunch, and I readily agreed.

We went to an Italian restaurant named Grisanti's that was famous for its fried ravioli! It was delicious!

The second day, nobody was in the office, so naturally I went back to Grisanti's!

I had been served my meal when I looked up and this absolutely gorgeous brunette woman was walking straight toward me with a big smile on her face!

I looked down, then back up, and she was even closer to me!

I noticed that she was dressed to the nines, and she was about three feet from me!

She had on a fur cape, and suddenly she opened it and said, "My dress is made out of such and such, and this fur cape is genuine fox!"

I felt my face turn red, and she started laughing!

I said, "Lady, I don't know what you're selling, but I'm buying!"

She said, "I'm a model in a fashion show. There are a lot of us here today."

I got up my courage and asked her what her name was, and she said, "Barbara Hummel!"

It turned out that she was Miss America in 1946! When she was single, it was Barbara Walker!

What a thrill!

MiG Alley

By Rudy Martin

I learned to love shooting diving ducks on little
Lennox Lake near Dumas, Arkansas.

We kill puddle ducks too, but scaup, ringnecks, redheads,
and canvasbacks accounted for most of our kill.

One year, we built a blind in the end of the lake nearest the
barrow pit, and we situated it back in the buckbrush.

The blind faced east, and there was a north/south lane about
twenty yards in front of the blind that extended both ways for
a couple of hundred yards. It was a perfect ambush spot.

The divers would spot our spread and roar in
from either direction to buzz the decoys.

The problem was that the buckbrush hid most of the lane from
view. You could only see a few yards north and south of the blind.

The Korean War was going on, and there was a lot in
the newspapers about MiG Alley, a place where US
F-86 saber jets tangled in dogfights with soviet MiGs
flown by North Korean and Chinese pilots.

I named this blind the MiG Alley blind, where
lightning-quick reflexes were a definite advantage.

I shot a Winchester Model 12 pump shotgun, and Dad
shot a Winchester Model 50 semiautomatic. Since both

of them were made by Winchester, the safety was in
the same place, and they had a very similar feel.

One morning, I was stirring a pot of soup mom had made us
when about ten or twelve divers appeared out of nowhere!

I dropped the spoon, grabbed the nearest gun, then neatly
folded a ringneck on my first shot. Not realizing it was Dad's
semiautomatic, I nearly jerked the forearm off it trying to pump it!

Dad saw what was happening and shouted, "It's mine! Shoot!"
I managed to knock down another one before they got out of range!

Like all young men, I had some habits that frustrated Dad,
but one related to that blind almost drove him crazy.

He had some red-and-white enamel metal cups we used to
drink our coffee. The drill was to put an old-time percolator
on the charcoal heater and let it brew the coffee.

Many times, I had one of those cups in my hand when
the ducks would suddenly appear. My norm was to
pitch the cup into the lake and grab a gun!

Dad pleaded with me for me to take the time
to set it down, but it was to no avail.

That's when Dad's frugality came into play. Evidently, there
was gold underneath that red-and-white enamel paint,
because nothing would do but for me to get in the boat
and fish the cup out of the water. Fortunately the water
was gin clear and relatively shallow, but it wasn't easy to
use a stick to scoop up the cup off the coontail moss.

That blind is definitely my favorite of all the blinds I've ever hunted.

Memories of My Grandfather's Shotgun

By Rudy Martin

I never knew my dad's father. He died when my dad was in the eleventh grade.

But Dad kept his shotgun, a Remington 12 gauge double-barrel with hammers, two triggers, and 33" barrels.

It looked just like the ones you see in Western movies, except for the longer barrels.

I never knew if it was Damascus steel. Dad kept it in the attic of the house I grew up in, in a gun case.

One New Year's Eve when I was about ten, Dad and several of his friends woke me up and got me to shoot it off the back porch at midnight.

The kick knocked me off the porch! Of course, they thought it was hilarious!

When I was in high school, my friends and I shot it a few times (low brass number 8 shot—I wasn't about to test the barrels with high brass loads).

The only thing I ever killed with it was a buzzard—a big no-no.

And so it remained in Dad's attic for over forty-five years, until Dad died in 1986. He left it to me in his will.

I brought it to my house and considered it a treasured heirloom. Some research indicated that it was only worth a few hundred dollars, but it was priceless to me.

Dad also left me four all brass 00 buckshot shells, and I visualized these and the shotgun in a glass display over my mantel.

Then in 1993, my house was burglarized, and it was taken along with several other guns, including two vintage Winchester Model 12 pumps! I had recorded all the serial numbers, but the police weren't interested in seeing them. They made only a token effort for recovery.

So, Mr. Burglar, I hope you put some Magnum shells in it and pulled the trigger. And I hope the barrels exploded and did you some serious damage! If you chose to pawn it, I hope it's a prized possession of someone who appreciates it.

Mary Jane

By Rudy Martin

I knew Mary Jane Melton in college. She was a superstar—president of the student body, president of her sorority, etc.

Years later, I ran into her at the Little Rock Racquet Club. She was as beautiful as ever!

She told me her son Robert was a good tennis player, and she needed a sponsor to join the club.

Of course I said I'd be glad to sponsor her, and I did.

I was living in a house in Leewood when she came over to my house and said that her father had bought the house across the street for her.

I was married to Liz at the time, and the three of us started spending a lot of time together.

We had lots of cookouts!

Things turned sour for Liz and me, and we got a divorce.

Mary Jane told me later that Liz came over to her house and said, "I'm warning you, Rudy will be over here after you," and I was!

We started dating and quickly fell in love. After a whirlwind courtship, we got married!

We were very well matched.

We liked to do the same things—attend performances at Robinson Auditorium, go to the River City Chorus performances, attend Christmas pageants, etc.

Then her obstetrician found a spot on her bladder, and it was cancer.

As expected, she fought the good fight but passed away.

I will always cherish the sixteen years we had together.

Martini

By Rudy Martin

This man was going into a very expensive restaurant to have lunch when a nun who was standing near the door said, "Sir, would this be a suitable place for me to eat lunch?" He said, "Well, yes, it is, Sister. In fact, I would be honored if you'd be my guest for lunch." She said, "Yes, I will, thank you."

They got seated, and the waiter said, "Would you like a cocktail?"

The nun said, "Do you have a drink menu?" The waiter handed it to her. She studied it a minute and said, "I'll have a martini, as in mar-ten-i." The man didn't want to embarrass the nun by pointing out that's not how it's pronounced, so he said to the waiter, "Two mar-ten-i's!" The waiter went to the bartender and said, "Two mar-ten-i's!" And the bartender said, "Is that damn nun in here again?"

Levee Drink

By Rudy Martin

This happened shortly after my sister and brother-in-law moved to Pine Bluff, Arkansas, when I was still living in Memphis working for IBM.

Dad, my brother-in-law, Teryl Brooks, and I spent a weekend fishing the barrow pit that runs into little Lennox Lake.

Dad said they call them barrow pits because the dirt from them was used to build the Arkansas River levee, and the dirt was moved by hand in wheelbarrows!

Everybody pronounces it "borrow," so I had always assumed that the name came from the dirt being "borrowed" from there to build the levee!

We caught a nice stringer of bass on Saturday afternoon, and we left the water and headed for the motel in Dumas.

Dad fixed us a drink. Teryl and I watched in amazement as he used an entire pint of bourbon to fix three drinks! You had to drive up on the Arkansas River levee on a grass road to get on top of the levee, so we dubbed the toddies "levee drinks."

Needless to say, we were feeling no pain when we reached the motel.

The restaurant there didn't have a liquor permit, but that didn't stop us from taking our drinks inside.

Maybe it was our loud talking, or maybe it was Dad's calling the waitress "seal beams" (she had on thick eyeglasses), but she took a dim view of our having those drinks in her restaurant!

Dad told her it was iced tea, but she said,
"I know what it is. I can smell it."

We weathered the storm of protest and managed to eat there, but forevermore "levee drinks" were etched in history!

King Henry IV

By Rudy Martin

My dad was the first person in Pine Bluff to have a Labrador Retriever. Dad got him from a kennel in Michigan.

A year later, a man got a black female lab, they bred them and she had eight puppies—four black and four yellow.

They were precious!

I chose a large yellow puppy and named him Rex.

A man in Pine Bluff liked to put on dog shows, and he called my dad and asked him if we would show off our labs at the show, and Dad said yes.

They had roped off an area in a building, and our labs were behind the rope.

When the show started, there were dogs passing by us.

There were some minor skirmishes between German Shepherds and Doberman Pinschers, but nothing serious.

The announcer announced that Mrs. Whodathunkit would now show her prize standard poodle King Henry IV.

He was the damnedest thing we had ever seen!

His head and ears had been shaved, there was a band of fur around his middle, his back legs had been shaved, and his tail had been shaved down to a pom-pom on the end!

As he passed by us, my dad said the unconscionable, "Fetch him up!"

All hell broke loose!

The labs lunged at him, and he jumped into Mrs. Whodathunkit's arms!
The icy stare from Mrs. Whodathunkit was something to behold!

Needless to say, we weren't invited back the next year!

Kate

By Rudy Martin

Kate came to Mary and I when she was a tiny little puppy.

She followed us everywhere. She was Mary's constant companion.

Mary told me about the time Kate guarded
her one night when she was scared!

She was an excellent chocolate Labrador
Retriever—the whole works!

She loved it when three of us hunted out of a blind
on Horseshoe Lake, near Sherrill, Arkansas.

Her favorite time of the hunt was about nine, when we
would all get out our ritz crackers and she would beg for
some, so you had to keep them out of her reach!

Periodically we would cripple a duck, and it
would go down on the opposite bank!

I would put Kate in my boat and paddle to the other side.
When the bow of the boat hit the bank, she would leap out
of the boat and start looking for that crippled duck!

She had an incredible nose!

Nearly every time, she'd come running back
to me with that duck in her mouth!

She lived fourteen years, then developed cancer and died!

Kate, both of us loved you with every bone in our bodies!

A lot of people believe that our dogs are waiting for us in heaven!
One day they'll catch our scent, stare intently, and then
run lickety-split into our arms and lick our face!

Then together we'll walk across the Rainbow Bridge,
and when we reach the other side, Kate will say,

"Welcome home!

Sleep tight!"

Jungle Party

By Rudy Martin

The SAEs had a "Jungle Party" each year in the spring.

When I was a senior, Bill Tedford, Jim Withem, and I went to the alligator farm on Mount Gaylor and asked the manager if we could borrow an alligator for our Jungle Party.

The manager said, "Sure, just bring him back the next day."

The engineers built a "waterfall" from the third floor to the basement, and the three of us tied him to a rock there.

Lots of students (girls and boys) got their picture taken with it.

The manager of the farm told us that the alligator would be dormant this time of the year because it was hibernating!

The three of us went upstairs to dance, and unbeknown to us, Charlie Ferguson had gotten a short stick and beaten the hell out of the alligator!

Bill got into the pool to adjust its rope when the alligator went nuts!

It was wriggling, hissing, and had its mouth wide open!

Bill lost control of one of its back feet, and Bill's arm grazed its teeth and drew blood!

Bill turned toward me. His arm was shaking, and he said, "He got me, he got me!"

I took him to the infirmary, and the nurse put some medicine and a bandage on it and said, "Of all the years I've been here, I've never treated a student for alligator bite!"

Jeans

By Rudy Martin

I recently sold my house and am living in a
very nice retirement community.

I've been tied up with some business things, and my daughter
graciously offered to move my things to the retirement home.

One morning, I decided to put on a clean pair of
jeans, but I didn't know where she put them.

I found three pairs in my chest of drawers
and took the pair on the top.

I had just gotten up, so I sleepily put both legs where
they go, and much to my surprise, they were way, way
too small—a hummingbird couldn't wear them!

I figured that my daughter was playing a
practical joke on me, so I called her.

She said she wasn't and to see what size the other two pairs were.

They both were my size!

It's a Shark

By Rudy Martin

One summer, my wife and I and our three kids spent a weekend on Petit Jean Mountain in Mather Lodge.

On Saturday morning, we went down to Cedar Falls, and that afternoon we went fishing on a small lake near the lodge.

I rented a johnboat and bought some crickets, and we started fishing with the cane poles I had brought.

We caught some small bream and warmouth perch, but nothing to write home about.

All of a sudden, Paula's cork went under, and when she raised her cane pole up, it bent almost double, and a large fish of some kind splashed around on the surface!

She let out a war whoop, and I scrambled to get the dip net!

I got her to lead the fish into the dip net, and I raised it up and put both the dip net and the fish in the boat!

It was a spotted gar that weighed at least five pounds! Paula yelled, "Look, it's a shark! Look at those teeth!" I told Paula it was not a shark. It was a gar. The kids started pleading with me to put it back in the lake before it bit somebody!

Fortunately I had a pair of long-nose pliers, got the hook out, and dropped him over the side of the boat.

On each of our fishing trips, Paula caught the odd fish—a catfish, drum, grinnel (bowfin), etc.—but this gar took the prize hands down!

It Don't Take Long

By Rudy Martin

A blacksmith had a young boy who liked to watch him work.

One afternoon, the blacksmith had just gotten a red-hot horseshoe out of the fire when the phone rang.

He used some tongs to get it out of the fire and sat it on a metal rack, then answered the phone.

He was on the phone for quite a while and had forgotten about the hot horseshoe!

When he got back, he saw it and foolishly picked it up with his gloved hand!

He dropped it and yelled, "Damn, that hurts! Damn, that hurts!"

The young boy said, "Dad, did you burn your hand?" And the dad said, "No, it just don't take me long to look at a horseshoe!"

In The Ribs

By Rudy Martin

The Episcopal Church my family went to had a Midnight Communion Service on Christmas Eve.

My dad and I always went duck hunting on my birthday, Christmas Eve.

We'd get back to town around noon and take a nap so we'd be fresh for it.

There's a place in the service where they turn all the lights down low, and it gets real quiet.

That's when Dad and I struggle to stay awake!

If my mother caught us napping, she would poke us in the ribs!

Ouch, that hurt!

I Can't Find It

By Rudy Martin

In the "no brakes" story, I told of the time my car had no brakes, crossed Arkansas Avenue, and ran into a metal net in a tennis court chain-link fence.

Since then, I've had a nightmare that my car is racing down that hill. I've fallen between the front seat and the dash and am frantically trying to stop the car with my hands on the pedals.

I was home for a weekend and went to sleep in my own twin bed. Mom woke Dad up and said that I was yelling, so Dad ran to my room to see what was going on.

Dad said that I had crawled off the foot of my bed and was under the bathroom sink banging on the wall and yelling, "I can't find it, I can't find it!"

Dad said he took me by the arm and said, "Come on, son, I know where it is."

He helped me get back in my bed, and everybody went back to sleep.

Hot Tamale Pies

By Rudy Martin

My grandmother Suzie Martin grew up in
Magnolia, Arkansas. It's a quaint little town.

I used to go over to her house in Pine Bluff and sit for
hours while she told me what life was like living there.

She was born before the turn of the century,
not long after the civil war ended.

She told me about the Scalawags and the Carpetbaggers.

Ms. Suzie was a feisty woman, in spite of the
fact that she was only five feet tall.

She lived with us for a while, then opened up a
country store in Bald Knob, Arkansas.

Then she moved back to Pine Bluff, bought a house,
and started making and selling hot tamale pies.

They were delicious, and folks clamored to get
them! There was even a waiting list for them.

She made them in a one-pound coffee can. She would put in
a layer of "mush," then a layer of meat, mushrooms, onions,
and her "secret" spices, then alternate the mush and meat
until the coffee can was full. She never used a recipe.

When you wanted to serve it, you got a pretty large
pot, filled it half full of water, put the coffee can
in the pot, and boiled it until it was hot.

They were delicious!

Unfortunately, she fell down the concrete steps that
lead to the street and broke both of her arms.

But not to worry, in a week, she was making
them again with both of her arms in casts.

She died when she was ninety-two, and in my mind, she's
making those hot tamale pies for the folks in heaven!

Ms. Suzie, I loved you with every bone in my body!

Sleep tight!

Hi, Frank

By Rudy Martin

My dad took my mother and me fishing one Sunday afternoon.

We had a boat on top of the car, and he and I
lifted it off and slid it into the water.

About that time, my mother said she had to pee, so we went and sat
down in the boat on the side opposite from the side Mom was on.

Dad gave my mother just enough time to get started when
he jumped up and said, "Hi, Frank! How are you?"

All the commotion made my mother pee in her
pants, and she didn't get over it for a long time!

There was no Frank!

Here's To Eve

By Rudy Martin

In 1964, I married Paula Hamm. She lived in Memphis, so we had the rehearsal dinner at the Racquet Club in Memphis.

We had a fine dinner—prime rib, scalloped potatoes, and lemon icebox pie for dessert!

It's customary for the father of the groom to make a toast after dinner.

So after dinner, my dad tapped on his glass of tea, and when things quieted down, said,

"Here's to Eve, the mother of our race, who wore a fig leaf in a most peculiar place. And here's to Adam, the father of us all, who was Johnny on the spot, when the leaves began to fall!"

He got a standing ovation!

Here We Go Loop-T-Loop

By Rudy Martin

One winter, my wife and I visited a ski lodge in Southern Missouri.

The name of it was Tan-Tar-A.

They had a hill that was packed with artificial
snow that everybody skied on.

We signed up for lessons, but they weren't satisfactory.

All I "kinda learned" to do was the snow plow.

I watched several take off, and none of them fell.

I got the big head and said, "Hey, man, that ain't no problem!"

I bent my knees and shoved off.

I made it down the slope fine, but I tensed
up when I saw grass ahead of me.

How in the hell do I stop?

I froze, and when I hit the grass, I hurtled out
of my skis and skidded on the grass!

Several people snickered at my flight!

Now how in the hell do I get back to the top of the hill?

I saw people on the left side of the hill being pulled
back up the hill by a rope, so I walked over there.

I stood to the side and watched several people
grab the rope, and away they went!

Again my ego said, "Hell, a blind man can do that!"

I got in line, and when my turn came, I let the
rope run through both hands, clamped down, and
immediately turned a complete somersault!

Several people had the gall to clap for me, so I gave them the finger!

I made it back to the top, but I still had no clue how to stop!

Obviously the thing to do was to take another snow
plow lesson, but my pride wouldn't let me!

What, "Jean Claude Keely" taking a lesson? Absurd!

I had an interesting trip my second trip down.

Everything was going great until a huge man had the
nerve to block my path and knock us both sprawling!

Turns out he was a starting linebacker for
the University of Missouri.

I pondered whether to admit that skiing wasn't my
sport, but again my pride got in the way.

On my third trip down, a storage building
"suddenly" appeared, and I plowed into it!

And on my fourth and final trip down, I encountered a chain-link fence, and I ran beside it for what seemed like a mile before I passed out!

So I went home and got back to the contact sports I knew I could do—jacks, tiddledywinks, charades, blackjack, hide-and-seek, etc.

I rarely have to go to the hospital when I've been playing these!

Green Peas

By Rudy Martin

My dad loved to watch the Gillette boxing show on TV every Friday night.

Four of us were at a cabin Dad had.

The TV was in the living room, and Dad was in the kitchen cooking supper.

His specialty was green peas.

Dad really got into boxing, and he would stand up and throw punches at the boxers.

"Get up, get up. Beat the count!"

Dad was throwing punches at the TV when his arm knocked the green peas pot off the stove!

The pot threw green peas all over the living room while we were doubled over with laughter!

I don't know what Dad said, but there were some canines mentioned!

Gravy

By Rudy Martin

I grew up in Pine Bluff, Arkansas. My sister is three years older than I am. Her name is Helen Claire—I'm Rudy!

We were eating supper in our breakfast room, and as usual, Helen Claire and I were bickering about some trivial thing.

My mother had a very calm disposition, but that day, she had taken all she could take!

Just as our maid, Sadie, was putting a full silver gravy boat on the table, my mother lost it with us!

She slammed her fist on the table. It hit the end of the gravy ladle and splashed gravy all over the ceiling!

Helen Claire and I knew it was time to get the hell out of Dodge, so we bolted for our bedrooms and locked the doors!

My mother was a very kind, sweet person, so in a few minutes, she went to the living room and in a soft voice, asked us to join her!

She was crying, and she repeatedly apologized for losing her temper!

Grab That Bass

By Rudy Martin

My dad, my son, and I were fishing Little Lennox Lake, which is near Dumas, Arkansas.

To put it bluntly, the bass were eating it up!

We were all fishing with a devil horse, a long floating bait with a propeller on each end.

Dad had taught us his rhythm. It was (1) let the ripples die, (2) give it a short jerk, (3) let the ripples die, and (4) give it a short jerk, etc.

We had an igloo cooler with us, and it was already full of really nice-sized bass.

All of a sudden, a huge bass jumped out of the water and pounced on my torpedo, and the fight was on! My son got the dip net under him and put him in the boat!

He got the hooks out, laid him in the cooler, and closed the lid!

To our horror, the bass gave a mighty flop, knocked the lid open, and we watched as the largest bass I have ever caught (about ten pounds) fell back in the water and disappeared!

I've had many dreams about that bass, and I'm convinced that when he joined his buddies, he said, "Guys, I thought it was all over, so I made one final leap and here I am!"

Gin and Frog

By Rudy Martin

Three of us decided we wanted to fish Crooked
Creek, the best smallmouth stream in the state.

Jerry McKinnis had put a drawing of Turkey Landing
in the paper, so we struck out to find it.

Of course, we got lost!

While we were searching, I spied a huge
bullfrog on the other side of a pond.

I showed it to the other guys, picked up a rock, and said,
"Y'all watch this," and it landed on top of his head!

I ran around to the other side of the pond and collected my prize!

I put him in our igloo cooler, and we continued
searching for Crooked Creek.

We gave up and drove to Yellville.

We stopped for gas when the "hunchback of
Notre Dame" came out to wait on us!

He told us that there was no Turkey Landing,
and we could put in at his house.

We followed him and got to his house.

We launched one johnboat and told him we would come back and get our car after the first boat reached the "taking-out place."

They would load their stuff into their car and wait for us.

It was a bright, sunny day.

I was in the second boat, and the fishing was good.

Out of nowhere, a violent thunderstorm appeared—lots of thunder and lightning!

It was raining cats and dogs!

We decided that the safest thing was to paddle straight through to the taking-out place!

We rounded a bend, and the guys from the first boat were standing under a tree, completely drenched!

Alwyn produced a bottle of gin and some cups, and we all got tiddly.

Alwyn had put the bullfrog in our igloo cooler, so we would put ice in our cups, pour gin into our cups, and drink away!

It tasted awful!

We paddled straight to the taking-out place, loaded up the first boat's gear, and headed for the hunchback's house!

When we got there, he came running to us and said we couldn't drive through his pasture because if we did, we would muddy it up!

We would have to leave the first car until it dried up!

So we headed for Harrison (we had reservations there).

We checked into our rooms, everybody took a hot shower,
only to find out that all of us were covered in ticks!

We slept in the next morning, then drove to Yellville.

The hunchback said that we could drive
the first car across his pasture!

We never did find Turkey Landing!

Fire at the House

By Rudy Martin

It was the Fourth of July, and several of Helen Claire's friends had gathered in our front yard.

As I recall, the girls who were there were Margie Snyder, Betty Ed Young, Millie Lee, Emily Sanders, and Barbara Pfeffer.

The boys who were there were Jimmy Higgason, Roy Edgington, Kayo Harris, Bill Reid, Jack Means, and others were shooting fireworks in the street in front of our house.

Our house had a flat roof over the sun porch.

One of the boys got the bright idea to throw sparklers over the front of the house and into the backyard!

Big mistake!
When Dad walked into the backyard, the sparklers were landing on the flat roof, and it was on fire!

He immediately called the fire department, but by the time they got there, the attic was on fire!

Early on, Dad had gone into the house and brought out only his shotgun!

Tomorrow was Helen Claire's birthday, so Mother went into the house and came out with the favors for her!

If that weren't enough, Dad and our boarder tried to get Munnie's baby grand piano out the front door!

Of course, it was too big to get out the door!

The firemen climbed up the stairs to the attic and began spraying the rafters, and pretty soon they had the fire under control!

I remember Dad, Mom, Helen Claire, and I
all standing on the sidewalk crying!

The damage wasn't too bad, although the rafters were charred.

Our family was very lucky that the damage wasn't worse!

Father-Daughter

By Rudy Martin

My daughter Paula and I played in several father-daughter tennis tournaments. Last year, we won the city and the state championships!

We qualified for the national father-daughter championship, which was held in Memphis.

We won two rounds, which put us in the finals of the national father-daughter championship.

Our opponents were a father and his daughter. Someone told us before the match that the father had played basketball for the Boston Celtics!

We met them at the net, and Paula and I were shocked that he was 6'10" tall!

No-ad tennis was played in all these tournaments!

I played in the deuce court, and Paula played in the ad court! The father played in the deuce court, and we quickly found out that he had a vicious topspin forehand!

We won the first set 6–4, and they won the second set 6–3!

Then we were tied at 4–4 in the third set when we broke the daughter's serve, making the score 5–4 us and me serving!

The game score was 5–5 with me serving!

That meant that whichever team won the next point would be the national father-daughter champions!

I had had some success lobbing the return over the daughter's head because the father was charging the net on every point, and I knew that if I could hit a good lob, we would be the national father-daughter champions!

I did hit a good lob, but the long-tall father was able to stretch out and get the ball in play to me, but I made an error, and they won the match 6–4, 6–5!

Close but no cigar!

Elvis

By Rudy Martin

I went to work for IBM in Memphis when I graduated from the University of Arkansas in Fayetteville, Arkansas.

I was looking for a place to live when I ran across a man named Jim Spurlock.

He was a cotton buyer on Front Street, and by chance, he was looking for three young men to share his house with him.

George Falls, who worked for Holiday Inn, Joe Pegram, who also worked for IBM, and I all moved into Jim's house with him. We named it the "batchelor's flat."

George had a friend in South Memphis who was renting an apartment in South Memphis, and there was a grass field beside it where we played touch football.

We were having lots of fun when a black limousine pulled over and stopped.

We were curious, so we stopped the game temporarily.

A man came over to us and said that he was Elvis Presley's bodyguard, and Elvis wanted to join us!

We said he was welcome, so he joined us.

It turned out that he was a very good athlete, and he had a great personality. He played with us for about an hour then left.

Can you believe that us country boys got to play football with

The King!

Ee's No Problem

By Rudy Martin

Gregor Tiriac was from Rumania. He was the tennis coach of Ilie Năstase, who reached number 5 in the world.

Gregor and Ivan Lendl became close friends.

At one time, Ivan was ranked number 1 in the world.

Ivan invited Gregor to spend the weekend with him in New York City.

As they were driving to Ivan's house, he told Gregor that he had two attack dogs in his house to protect him, and he said that if you do something wrong, they will attack you.

Gregor said, "Ee's no problem!"
Ivan told him that when he opened the door, he was not to look at either dog or he would be attacked.

Again Gregor said, "Ee's no problem."

When Ivan opened the door, the dogs bristled at Gregor. He said something to them in Rumanian, and both dogs ran to the back of the house.

So again Gregor said, "Ee's no problem!"

Dress Code

By Rudy Martin

Men who work for IBM have a very rigid dress code—Florsheim wing tip shoes, a three-piece suit with a vest, no flat top, etc.

Do you know how to spot an IBMer getting on an airplane?

His fly will be open.

Dorm Guard

By Rudy Martin

I was taking boot camp at Lackland Air Force Base in San Antonio, Texas. It lasted eight weeks.

All military bases station a serviceman at the front door of every barracks. Nobody is allowed to enter without the proper credentials.

I was assigned to be the dorm guard the third day we were there.

On a side note, when I was in high school I spent three eight-week summers at Culver Summer School in South Bend, Indiana.

The US Navy sponsored it, so we wore navy uniforms and marched everywhere we went.

Over three summers, I learned to row, sail, memorize the navy flags, learn semaphore, and plot courses on Lake Michigan (I was only in the ninth grade and that took a knowledge of trigonometry).

I also became a damn good tennis player when I was there!

It was a wonderful opportunity for me.

Back to the air guard base.

I had heard that a crusty staff sergeant was tough on dorm guards, so I was ready when he showed up!

He said, "Goddamn it, airman, let me into those barracks!"

I said, "Sir, I need to see your credentials, sir!"

He said, "I don't need any GD Credentials, open that GD door!"

I said, "No, sir!"

He berated me for about fifteen minutes, smiled, and said, "Good job, airman!"

Hooray for Culver!

Don't Drop It

By Rudy Martin

One morning, I fell into the white river holding a 7 1/2HP outboard motor. It was just at daylight, and I was stepping from a boat dock into a johnboat!

Just as I committed to stepping, waves made by another boat caused the johnboat to rise above the dock. My toe ended up hitting the side of the boat. I lost my balance and plunged into the river between the boat dock and the johnboat!

The weight of the motor plummeted me to the bottom, and I pushed off it and popped to the surface for a second, gasping for air! Of course, the motor pulled me right back under, and I pushed off again!

Dad said I looked like a porpoise as I suddenly appeared and disappeared on my downstream journey!

As this was going on, Dad's imagined words were ringing in my ears—

"Don't let go of that motor!"

He finally grabbed me by the shirt on about my fifth appearance.

I still had the motor—and a peeled shin to go with it!

Dogs Catching Fish

By Rudy Martin

When I was in the eighth grade, Little Lennox Lake and its attached bar pit dried up almost completely. Dad and I tried to duck hunt the lake, but there was just a puddle of water left. Rex, my yellow lab, and I decided to check out the barrow pit. It was also down to a fraction of its original size, to about fifty yards wide by one hundred yards long.

The water depth ranged from about two feet down to a few inches. A lot of fish were rolling in the muddy water, and I shot a spotted gar about two feet long with my shotgun. Being trained to retrieve, Rex jumped in and brought him to me. I shot another one with the same result.

Then Rex brought me one that hadn't been shot. I sicced him in the water, and he brought me two more. Knowing that Dad would hear the shooting, I knew he would join me. He shot a drum, and Shag, his black lab, retrieved it. Rex showed up with another gar, Shag caught a crappie, and it was on!

After they caught about twenty fish, Dad said we were going to Pine Bluff and bring back some photographers to record this event for posterity.

The next day, we had Mr. Dick McGill with a 16 mm movie camera and Henry Marks with a still camera.

The film was awesome, containing among other things a breathtaking scene of Shag catching a five-pound bass!

Rex continued to specialize in gar.

Dad showed the film all over Pine Bluff (Rotary, Kiwanis, Lion's Club, etc.). He was even featured on Bud Campbell's sports show on Channel 7. Bill Roberts, a friend of Dad's, had it transferred to video before Dad died, and I have it.

Sic 'em, dogs!

Dog

By Rudy Martin

A man was standing on a street corner with
a big dog sitting beside him.

A stranger walked up to him and said, "Does your dog bite?"

The man said, "No," but when the stranger reached
down to pet him the dog nearly took his arm off!

The stranger said, "I thought you said your
dog didn't bite," and the man said,
"That ain't my dog."

Do He Hunt Squirrels?

By Rudy Martin

When I was living in Memphis, my friend Jim Spurlock invited me to go dove hunting on the opening day of the season.

I had my Labrador Retriever Sam with me. He was fully trained, whistle, hand signals—the full package.

There were lots of hunters there, and we were spaced about seventy-five yards apart.

I killed my limit of twelve, but I missed some easy shots.

I was getting ready to leave when I saw two men walking around in circles, obviously looking for dead doves.

I decided that I'd show them what a cream-of-the-crop dog could do.

I walked over to them and said, "Good morning, guys. Looks like you could use some help."

They said, "Yes we could. There are six dead doves right around here."

I told Sam to "find it, find it!"

In short order, Sam found all of them, and one of them said, "Do he hunt squirrels too?"

I contained my laughter and said, "No, he's a duck dog!

Only feathers!"

Dean Martin

By Rudy Martin

When Dean Martin had his own show, the audience thought the drink cup he held was water, but it was straight gin!

A man in the cast loved to play practical jokes on Dean. His name was Ken Lane. He had his piano made of balsa wood!

Dean sang love songs, and Dean always jumped up on Ken Lane's piano and sang love songs. When Dean jumped up on it, since it was made of balsa wood, it shattered into a million pieces!

Dean just laughed!

Dead Battery

By Rudy Martin

When our kids were young, we used a babysitter named Flossie. She lived in a rough part of town near UAPB.

When I took her home, I always took my black lab, Sam, with me. You never knew if something would happen.

There were no streetlights where Flossie lived, and it was spooky!

We rounded a corner, and a late-model car was blocking the street.

I pulled up behind it, and after a couple of minutes, I blinked my lights.

No response!

I waited a couple of minutes More and blinked my lights again!

No response!

In desperation, I honked my horn!

All four doors flew open and four young black men got behind it and started pushing it!

They pushed it about a block, and the motor started!

They all jumped in it and drove away!

Apparently their battery was dead!

Man, that was spooky!

Danger

By Rudy Martin

I was in high school and was taking Sally Miller to the Sanger theater to see a movie. It was misting rain.

To get to the theater, we had to walk (on the sidewalk) right by the Western Union office.

When I got to Western Union, I noticed that there was a solid-black Cadillac parked there, and one of the back windows was down about six inches. I thought that I would be a good Samaritan and roll the man's window up.

But when I stepped off the sidewalk, I was greeted by a snarling, out-of-control Doberman Pinscher that wanted a piece of me!

Fortunately, he was way too big to fit through the crack in the window, so Sally and I skedaddled to the theater!

As soon as I got her seated, I went to the men's room and threw up.

I was calmed down when the movie was over, but I dreaded walking by that Cadillac again!

I told Sally to stand in front of the theater, and I would pick her up!

But the second I approached it, the Doberman was up in a flash, trying to get through the crack in the window!

Sally and I were two teenagers in love, but that night, I didn't even kiss her good night!

Talk about scared!

Cottonmouth

By Rudy Martin

Dad, Robert Fikes, and I spent a week camped on the bank
of Midway Lake, which is near Clarendon, Arkansas.

The bass were small—about one to two pounds,
but the crappie and redears were huge!

Dad had borrowed a mosquito bar tent.

It was so much cooler than a tent with canvas sides.
We put it up under some trees, and it was cool in
there except for the hottest part of the day.

Dad had built a live-box at home, and he tied it to a tree. It had
a wood frame and was covered with chicken wire all around it.

There was a hinged lid that let us get to the fish.

We were catching a lot of fish.

Every couple of days, we would take enough for supper.

They were delicious!

When we got ready to go to bed, Dad had a flit-
gun that had "skeeter scoot" in it.

That took care of the skeeters.

On the third night, Dad turned on his flashlight and
saw a gaping hole in the mosquito netting!

Mosquitoes were pouring through that hole!

Dad lit the Coleman lantern, and that helped some.

Fortunately Dad had a heavy-duty sewing kit, and he sewed the gap closed.

About that time, I discovered I was covered in mosquito bites!

At that age I was a very restless sleeper.

Sometimes I would get restless and get out of my bed and wander through the house.

Dad figured out I did indeed have one of my spells and ripped that hole.

One night, Dad was going to fry fish for our supper, and he got a bucket and headed for the live box.

It was dusk, so he took his flashlight.

In about five minutes, I heard him yell something. I didn't understand what he was saying, so I yelled, "What?"

He yelled, "Bring the rifle, bring the rifle!"

I grabbed my rifle and a flashlight and raced to him!

A huge cottonmouth moccasin was in the live well eating our fish!

All of a sudden, he started coming out of the live box and toward us!

I told Dad to back way up, and I would take care of him!

My rifle had a telescopic sight on it, but I couldn't see the crosshairs!

I turned the flashlight on, and that did the trick—I put three long rifle hollow point bullets in his head!

That was a scary experience!

Cinders

By Rudy Martin

When I was in High School, I worked after school and on Saturdays for a store that sold Office Supplies.

Late one afternoon, a woman came in, and I said, "Hi. What can I help you with?"

She said, "I want a box of cinders."

My mind went blank. All I could think of was the cinders on a running track!

The dadgum guys in the back started sniping at me with catty comments—"Do you eat 'em?" "What color are they?" "Do you buy 'em by the dozen?" Etc. Etc. Etc.!

Of course, I couldn't laugh in her face, so I knelt down below the counter and bit my tongue to keep my composure!

I could see the guys in the back, and I shushed them.

That didn't work so I gave them the finger!

That just made things worse!

I didn't dare raise up, so I started picking up random things and putting them on the counter—staplers, rubber bands, magic markers, paper weights, etc.!

She kept saying, "No, no, no, no," until I put a box of parcel post labels up there and she yelled, "Yes, that's what I want!"

I recovered my composure, and she said, "Those are what I use to send packages in the mail."

Anybody would know that!

Christmas Pine

By Rudy Martin

Growing up, my dad took me to cut a Christmas tree about ten days before Christmas.

He always let me pick it out, and he used a small axe to cut it down.

He had a stand for the tree, and it was always in our living room.

Dad, my mother, my sister, and I had fun hanging lights and Christmas balls on its branches. Then we topped everything off by draping tinsel over it. The wonderful smell of that pine tree permeated the whole house!

Dad always waited until we were asleep to assemble the moving gifts that were for me.

Waking up and running into the living room to see what we got was strictly forbidden! Dad made us eat breakfast beforehand!

He would stand in the hallway and close the door to the living room. Then he would go in the living room and get all of the toys moving, then he would say, "Okay!"

I'll always remember those Christmases!

A Christmas Eve Tradition

By Rudy Martin

My dad and I always went duck hunting on
Christmas Eve. That's my birthday.

Dad called me the night before and said he
was sick and for me to go alone.

It was a day of one calamity after another!

It was raining cats and dogs when I left
the house, but I went anyway.

When I arrived, I got stuck in the parking lot, which meant I
would have to find somebody with a tractor to pull me out.

Dad belonged to a hunting club that leased
about one hundred acres of green timber.

We kept a boat and motor in the deep water beside
the levee, so I struck out for the far end of the
reservoir, where I saw a lot of ducks working.

Of course, I was looking into the air when all of a sudden, the boat
hit something, turned somewhat sideways, and started taking water!

I shut the motor off and stepped onto a big
stump that was just under the surface!

The water in the boat made it turn over, dunking the motor!

So there I was—safe and sound but stranded on a stump!

Nobody else hunted that day.

I knew that Dad would come looking for
me, but that would be hours away.

The bank was about the length of the boat away, and I had
the bright idea of swiveling the bow of the boat around
and walking on the bottom of the boat to the bank.

I had waders on, and I prayed to the man
upstairs to not let me drown!

I took only one step when it tilted and I slid off!

To my surprise, the water was only about waist deep!

I shouted, "Thank you, Lord, for saving me!" and
crawled onto the bank on my hands and knees!

I was able to tilt the boat partially on its side
and drained the water out of it.

Now all I had to do was walk down the bank to where I was stuck.

Out of the corner of my eye, I saw some movement,
and it was a drake mallard flying by me!

I half-heartedly called at him, and he locked his wings and headed
straight for me, in spite of the fact that the boat was turned over
with the lower unit showing, and the red gas can was showing!

But here he came, so I loaded my gun
and folded him with one shot!

I sat on the boat and cried for a while, then said, "Thank you, Lord, for saving me.

The only thing having a worse day than I am is that drake mallard!"

Bald of My Back Head

By Rudy Martin

I had told my wife how beautiful the mountains around Petit Jean Mountain are in the fall, so we made a trip up there one Sunday afternoon. Sure enough, God was showing us his fall colors.

My daughter Paula got married in the chapel of the Episcopal Church summer camp. It's a beautiful chapel.

She looked so beautiful in her bridal gown. I cried all the way down the aisle!

The photographer had a picture of us walking down the aisle. I had it framed, and it sits on my desk.

I showed it to my wife and remarked how bald the back of my head was.

Except those weren't the words that came out of my mouth!

I said, "Look how that shows the bald of my back head!"

My dad would have said, "Son, you got your murds wixed!"

About the Author

Rudy Martin Jr. is an eighty-four-year-old outdoorsman who lives in Little Rock, Arkansas.

He graduated with honors from the University of Arkansas. After college, he worked for IBM for five years, had his own computer business for twelve years, then did computer work for Stephens Inc., an investment banking firm for twenty years.

His stories took place in Arkansas, Tennessee, Utah, and Canada.

Some are sad, some are funny, some are harrowing, some will make you feel good, with a few jokes thrown in. He has the uncanny ability to paint the scene for the reader—a poisonous snake, a vicious dog, an unruly toddler, a romantic week at Yellowstone, trying to learn how to ski, etc.

His passions are duck and goose hunting, fishing, and training field trial Labrador Retrievers.

His sense of humor will become apparent as you read through the book.

He loves to hunt and fish with his family and friends. His favorite day to duck hunt is when it is sleeting like crazy.

His three favorite dogs were Kate, Sam, and Jake, and there are multiple stories about them. They were part of his family.